American Shrines in England

American Shrines
in England

Bernadine Bailey

South Brunswick and New York: A.S. Barnes and Company
London: Thomas Yoseloff Ltd

A. S. Barnes and Co., Inc.
Cranbury, New Jersey 08512

Thomas Yoseloff Ltd
Magdalen House
136-148 Tooley Street
London SE1 2TT, England

Library of Congress Cataloging in Publication Data

Bailey, Bernadine Freeman, date
American shrines in England.

Includes index.
1. Historic sites—England. 2. Historic buildings—
England. 3. United States—History. 4. Great Britain
—History. I. Title.
DA660.B15 1976   942   75-20586
ISBN 0-498-01727-3

Printed in the United States of America

Contents

To
My very dear friend
Jill Knight, M.P., MBE
who is doing so much to promote
closer Anglo-American relations
and understanding.

Foreword

To most Americans and Canadians, a visit to England gives a sense of "coming home," regardless of strictly genealogical ties. As the cultural home of all English-speaking people, Britain offers a feast of "goodies" for all those who treasure the contributions of past centuries and persons long gone. To see the English background of these people helps to broaden one's understanding of North America as well as one's appreciation of the culture and way of life that England brought to the Western Hemisphere.

Semi-annual visits to England, over a period of twenty years, enabled the author to acquaint herself, and photograph, the places of special American interest that are described in this book. In the course of her trips to England, she attended the special ceremonies held at Runnymede in 1965 and at Plymouth in 1970. In 1971 she moved to London and lived there for three years, doing further research on Anglo-American ties. Her own ancestors, named Freeman, came to America from Isleworth, a suburb of London, in the year 1765.

Acknowledgments

The author wishes to express her sincere appreciation to the following persons for their assistance in obtaining the information and photographs in this book: Mrs. Doris Chesterton, Mr. and Mrs. Arthur Cooper, Rev. Peter R. Ince, Mrs. Angela James, Mrs. Jill Knight, M.P., Mrs. Heather McConnell, David Nealy, Mrs. Nora Simmons, and Canon Richard Tydeman.

American Shrines in England

A replica of Drake's ship, the *Golden Hind*, now anchored in San Francisco Bay.

1

The Age of Exploration: Drake and Raleigh

Devonshire, the land of Drake and Raleigh, has been described by many as the most beautiful county in England. Others say that no county has greater variety. No doubt both statements are true. It is equally true that Devon gave the world two of the greatest men of the sixteenth century—Sir Francis Drake and Sir Walter Raleigh, both of whom played a decisive role in the settlement of America.

It is no accident that some of Britain's greatest explorers came from this county in southeastern England. Its coastline is crinkled with bays, inlets, and harbors—a natural gathering place for ships and the men who sailed them. For that matter, there is no spot in all England that is more than 75 miles from the sea. But in Devon, almost everyone lived near the ocean or at least beside a river that led to the sea. Boys growing up were drawn to it like a magnet, for the sixteenth century was an age of adventure, of searching for lands beyond the seas. The exploits of such Portuguese explorers as Diaz and Vasco da Gama and such Spanish adventurers as Colombus, Balboa, Ponce de Leon, Cortez, and Pizarro were very much in people's minds. There was scarcely a lad living along the coast of Devon who didn't long to go to sea, perhaps hoping that he too might discover a new continent, an un-known river, or a far-away island. Many did go to sea as pirates or privateers, for these practices were

also widespread in the fifteenth and sixteenth centuries.

Devonshire produced more than a normal share of the great men of the sea, including Drake, Raleigh, Sir John Hawkins, Sir Humphrey Gilbert, and Sir Richard Grenville.

Sir Francis Drake was born in a cottage at Crowndale Farm, about a mile from Tavistock, Devon, in 1539. Tavistock is an ancient market town beside the Tavy River, about fifteen miles north of Plymouth. The original house no longer stands, but a tablet has been erected to mark the place where it stood. A statue of Drake stands at the entrance to Tavistock from the Plymouth road, at the west end of the town.

Drake came from good yeoman stock, and his father was a zealous Puritan and preacher. When Drake was twenty-three, he joined his cousin, John Hawkins, to learn the business of Atlantic voyaging. Hawkins took young Drake with him to the Gulf of Mexico, and Drake soon developed an undying hatred of the Spaniards, Britain's greatest rival, a feeling that was common among the English of that time. They resented Spain's monopoly of the lands and riches of South America. Actually, Hawkins himself was a buccaneer whose exploits had won favor with the Queen and the admiration of the younger generation.

When Drake was twenty-five, he was given a

regular privateering commission from Queen Elizabeth. When in command of the *Judith,* in 1567, Drake demonstrated his seamanship and daring against the Spaniards in the Gulf of Mexico. He harrassed the Spaniards and plundered their settlements in the West Indies, and his ship was one of two to escape destruction. On one such expedition, in 1572, Drake plundered his way across the Isthmus of Panama and thus became the first English commander to see the Pacific Ocean. He climbed a tree to get a better view, and the sight of this vast ocean made a tremendous impression. It fired his ambition and he vowed he would one day sail across this sea and find out what lay beyond it.

Shortly before this trip, however, when he was thirty years old, Francis Drake married Mary Newman on July 4, 1569, in St. Budeaux Church, near Plymouth. The young bride saw little of her husband, however, for almost from the day of his marriage he was constantly at sea.

Drake returned from the Gulf of Mexico on August 9, 1575, and shortly afterward was presented to the Queen. He hold her of his ambition regarding the Pacific and presented the idea so convincingly that she supplied the means for him to carry it out.

After serving in Ireland from 1573 to 1576, Drake returned to Devon and outfitted five ships. On December 13, 1577, he sailed out of Plymouth Harbor with this fleet of five small vessels and 166 men. Even the largest ship was hardly as big as a channel schooner. He sailed straight for the Straits of Magellan, where his fleet had to buck winds and currents. During a severe storm, one vessel sank with all hands on board, and the others were scattered. Drake renamed his flagship *Pelican* and called it the *Golden Hind.* He sailed along the coasts of Chile and Peru, sacking one Spanish town after another. Finally, with a ship full of treasure, he sailed northeast, seeking a passage to the Atlantic. Unable to find one, he was forced to turn back, but he stopped on the California coast to refit his ship. He called the land New Albion and claimed it for Queen Elizabeth.

Some historians claim that Drake never entered the Bay of San Francisco, which is almost invisible from the sea unless one is looking for it. It is certain, however, that he did land at another bay, the one named for him that lies some thirty miles west-by-northwest of the Golden Gate. Whether or not he entered the bay, San Francisco has always felt a special kinship with the great English navigator who was undoubtedly the first European to sail along the California coast.

On July 26, 1579, Drake left California and set out across the Pacific, reaching Java on March 11, 1580. After a short stay he started on his return voyage to England, reaching Plymouth on September 26, 1580. He had been gone nearly three years, and had become the first Englishman to voyage around the world. He had sailed through the Straits of Magellan and found untold plunder on the west coast of Spanish America, coming home through the East Indies and around the Cape of Good Hope. When he returned to Plymouth, his wife Mary rowed out with the Mayor of the city to greet her husband.

Sir Francis Drake was now a famous man, with immense wealth. He became mayor of Plymouth the next year and later a member of Parliament. In 1581, he bought the magnificent Buckland Abbey, a few miles north of Plymouth. This Abbey had been founded in 1273 as a retreat for the Cistercian monks. The previous owner, Sir Richard Grenville, had converted it into an impressive home, carving his house out of the church itself, putting three floors between its soaring walls and making them into living rooms. Cutting down the old kitchen, which was some distance from the church, he built a new wing to house the kitchen and domestic quarters. The great hall is the heart of the house, and the plaster frieze that runs the length of the west wall portrays an interesting allegory. It shows a soldier who has turned his war horse loose and hung his shield upon a tree, while he sits in meditation at its foot beside those well known symbols of mortality—the skull and the hourglass.

Buckland Abbey is still standing and is well worth a visit. It has become a shrine to Sir Francis Drake, containing many paintings and memorials of Drake and his descendants who have lived there. It remained in the Drake family until 1948. The architecture is nowhere ostentatious or ornate, but relies on mass and strength for its beauty. The name "Buckland" comes from "bocland," or land entered in the book. The Drake Room, the Georgian Room, and the Folk Gallery contain many mementos, banners, and paintings of great historical interest. The low, square tower, which is a distinctive feature of Buckland Abbey, was at one time used for housing pigeons.

A replica of the *Golden Hind* in Brixham Harbor, Devonshire, England.

When Drake came to live at Buckland, he was red-bearded and quick-tempered, a hardened seaman, resolute and impulsive in action, yet able to manage great affairs. Though he had known poverty and the keen discomfort of seafaring, he came to love fine clothes and the display of wealth. At the same time, however, he was a pious man, and read prayers twice a day when at sea. Buckland was ideally suited for him and his family, with even a bowling green for his amusement. The estate that went with the house, however, was not great, so Drake bought more land, in addition to what was given to him by the Queen in 1582.

Drake's first wife, Mary Newman, enjoyed the splendor of Buckland for only two years. After her death, Drake married the Court lady, Elizabeth Sydenham. For nearly ten years, Buckland was a country retreat from great affairs of State and the sea. When Drake fell into disfavor after the ill-starred expedition against Cadiz, in 1589, the Abbey became more like a prison. Yet it was still his great house, and here his treasures remained to honor his memory.

The Tithe Barn, 154 feet long, 28 feet wide, and 40 feet high, gives some idea of the rich harvests which the Cistercian monks won from their land. Since 1951, when Buckland was opened to the public, plays have been staged in the Tithe Barn.

In 1585, Drake returned to the sea and commanded a fleet of twenty-five ships in a plundering expedition in the West Indies. From there, he went to Florida and sailed up the coast to Virginia, where he saved the English colonists from annihilation at Roanoke. He returned to England in 1586, bringing tobacco and potatoes, both of which were new products to all Europeans.

Restless when on land, Drake was soon at sea again. Sailing this time with a fleet of thirty ships, he entered the bay of Cadiz, Spain, on April 19, 1587, and burned thirty-three Spanish vessels. Drake was later to refer to this victory as "singeing the King of Spain's beard."

When the Spanish Armada threatened England, in 1588, Drake was again called into service and was made vice-admiral of the fleet. There is a tradition that, when news came to Plymouth that the Armada was in sight, Sir Francis Drake insisted on finishing his game of bowls before going out to his ship. He and Hawkins sailed from Plymouth Sound with 190 men to defeat the Spanish Armada. In 1595, Drake commanded an unsuccessful expedition against the Spaniards in the West Indies, and on this trip he died aboard his ship, at the age of fifty-six. Presumably, he was buried at sea.

Plymouth has good reason to be grateful to Sir Francis Drake. Not only was he a splendid navigator, but he was an equally efficient surveyor. It was he who constructed the reservoir from the river Medway, which still supplies the city, and without which it could never have grown. In appreciation, at the annual inspection of the Waterworks by the Corporation of Plymouth, his memory is still toasted. Plymouth has honored its one-time mayor and great explorer by erecting a large statue of Drake on the Hoe, a large open space overlooking Plymouth Sound, from which he sailed on so many memorable occasions. The statue shows him looking out to sea.

Drake had brought riches and success back to the old seaport city, and when the people of Plymouth heard of his homecoming, after his round-the-world venture, they left their vicar preaching to an empty church and went to greet him.

In Roman and Phoenician times, there were very productive tin mines around Plymouth. Drake brought back gold and silver from the New World, and thus began a new era for the old seaport town. The riches brought back by Drake's fleet after conquering the Spanish Armada paved the way for the building of many new streets and houses, especially around the harbor. It was here that the rich merchants and seamen made their homes, many of which are still standing.

A replica of his famed flagship *Golden Hind* is anchored in Brixham Harbor, and it is well worth a visit. Another full-sized replica of the *Golden Hind* was launched in Appledore, England, in the spring of 1973. After several sea trials and long visits to Plymouth and the Thames, in London, the ship sailed for San Francisco in August of 1974. There it will remain as a floating museum and a permanent memorial to the first Englishman to drop anchor on the California coast.

East Budleigh, which lies two miles north of the seaside town of Budleigh-Salterton, in the Otter Valley, is a typical Devon village of thatched cottages with cob walls. In times gone by, it was an important wool-weaving center, when Budleigh-Salterton was only a small village.

Hayes Barton lies one mile west of East Budleigh, on the lower slopes of Woodbury Common. In this lovely old farmhouse, Sir Walter Raleigh was born, in 1552. A path leads up to the main door of the house through a typical English garden, and the fine old oak door, heavily studded with nails, is typical of the solid construction of the whole building. The visitor goes through a downstairs room and mounts stairs which were cut by hand from an oak tree without any of the precision, pattern, or measurements which would be used today. The local craftsman finished the tread of the stairs with his axe and as the planks came, so they were used. As a result, every tread is a different width.

The room in which Raleigh was born is a spacious chamber with a window looking over to Hayes Wood. Here again the floor boards vary in width and length just as they came from the tree. Set into the window is Raleigh's coat-of-arms. This was done following a suggestion made by the Duke of Windsor, who visited the house when he was Prince of Wales.

Many years ago an American, after a visit to Hayes Barton, was eager to purchase the house and offered to pay any price. He wanted to remove it stone by stone and set it up in Virginia. Needless to say, his offer was not even considered.

The house is E-shaped and has many old features. The front of the house has three gables between the main wings and a fine thatched roof. A letter in which Raleigh states that he was born in this house is in the Albert Memorial Museum at Exeter, and a replica of the letter hangs in the house.

Hayes Barton is a typical Devonshire farmhouse, now occupied by a farmer and his family, who show certain rooms to visitors. There are stone chimneys and the roof is thatched with Norfolk reed. The "E" shape was common in the sixteenth century, houses being built in this way as a compliment to Queen Elizabeth. The house is extremely picturesque, with cob walls on a stone foundation.

Raleigh's father was a country gentleman of old family but reduced means. He was married three times, Walter being the son of the third wife. She had formerly been married to a Mr. Gilbert, and one of her sons by this marriage was Sir Humphrey Gilbert, who planted the first English colony in North America and was drowned on his way home.

Nearby is the fifteenth-century church where Raleigh's father was a warden. This Church of All Saints contains many memorials to the Raleigh family. The family arms appear on the first pew to the left of the middle aisle. All the pew ends are carved, but they are unusual in that they depict secular subjects, such as vivid scenes of great adventure on the high seas. The pews are made of solid oak, three to four inches thick, and aged to a delightful dark color. They were probably carved by local men, and the subjects fall into three categories: (1) the arms of the local families; (2) emblems or allusions to local trades and occupations, such as ships, or shears for the wool trade; and (3) general ornamental designs. The Raleigh pew is dated 1537.

There is a small stained-glass window in the chancel of the church, in memory of Vice-Admiral George Wilson Preedy, who laid the first Atlantic cable uniting Europe to America in 1858. It is an interesting coincidence that these two men should be memorialized in the same church: the one who founded the first British colony in the New World and the one who completed the union between the Old and the New World.

In August, 1951, a tablet of oak, surmounted by Raleigh's coat-of-arms, was given by Dr. and Mrs. C.J.N. Longridge and unveiled in the church by the Bishop of Exeter. The tablet reads as follows:

Raleigh was born in this house, Hayes-Barton, near the village of East Budleigh.

Amore et Virtute

1552   1616

Sir Walter Raleigh was born at Hayes Barton in the Parish of East Budleigh, and in boyhood worshipped in this church, where his father was a churchwarden.

There has been a church on this site for more than eight hundred years. It was given by King Henry II to the Priory and Convent of Polslo in 1188, and parts of it were much older than that date. In 1433, part of it was rebuilt by Bishop Lacy, whose coat-of-arms may be seen on the easternmost window of the north aisle.

One bench end near the font bears the arms of the Conant family, who were neighbors of the Raleighs. Roger Conant was born here in 1592 and sailed to the New World three years after the Pilgrims, in 1623. He founded the Massachusetts Bay Colony.

Near the shallow step by the Raleigh pew lies the tomb of Joan Raleigh, first wife of Walter Raleigh's father.

The old vicarage, where Raleigh received his earliest education, is on the road to Hayes Barton and is full of hiding places and secret passages, for it was once the home of the smuggling parsons.

Young Raleigh quite literally grew up with a taste of the sea in his mouth. The pebbled beach of Budleigh-Salterton has probably changed very little in the four hundred years since young Walter Raleigh played here as a boy. The painter who immortalized the scene, Sir John Millais, was born in a strange little octagonal house at the west end of the road along the sea front. It was on the sea front of Budleigh-Salterton that Millais painted his most famous picture, "The Boyhood of Raleigh." It shows the young Raleigh and his half-brother, Humphrey Gilbert, listening to an old mariner's tale. The two boys in the picture were actually Millais' own two sons, and the old sailor was a local ferryman. The brilliant and effective coloring and the delicacy of the flesh tones make it outstanding. This painting was shown at the Royal Gallery in London in 1870 and was originally purchased for about £800 (then worth about $4,000). The buyer would never allow it to be photographed for reproduction. On his death, however, it was bought by Mrs. Tate for £5,460 (then worth about

$27,000) and presented by her to the Tate Gallery, where it may be seen today.

Raleigh's first real fighting was in the cause of the French Huguenots. It is said that he was in Paris during the Massacre of St. Bartholomew, and that this made an indelible impression. In any case, six years later he sailed as captain of a ship with his half-brother, Humphrey Gilbert, on an expedition against the Spaniards. This was not successful, so Walter went up to London to seek his fortune. Tall and handsome, with elegant manners and a quick wit, he had the qualifications that enable an unattached young man to go far, socially and politically—and he did.

At first, he was attached to the household of the Earl of Leicester, who introduced him at Court in 1581. Young Raleigh soon became a favorite of the Queen. He must have been a splendid figure, six feet in height, magnificently proportioned, handsome, and commanding. Queen Elizabeth was twenty years older than he and increasingly susceptible to the flattery of handsome young men. She gave him Durham House in 1583, knighted him in 1584, and showered him with properties and gifts until the Earl of Essex replaced him as her favorite. It may be only a legend that he spread his best coat over a puddle to keep the Queen from soiling her shoes, but in any case he had the sort of charm and manners that could well lead to such an act.

In addition to his great charm as a courtier, Walter Raleigh had a wealth of talents as a navigator, a poet, and a philosopher. He was also a successful agriculturist, an inventor, a statesman, and an historian. He personified the versatility and range of interest found in the Elizabethan Age. Although most of his poetic work was lost, more than twenty authentic poems by Raleigh were collected in 1891 and published by George Bell. Most people know little of Raleigh's writing except the line scratched on the glass window of the Queen's chamber: "Fain would I climb, yet fear I to fall." To which Her Majesty replied, "If thy heart fails thee, climb not at all."

Raleigh's interest in establishing colonies in the western world was aroused by his older half-brother, Humphrey Gilbert, who tried to find the Northwest Passage. Raleigh, however, was interested in the more southern areas, particularly what is now the coast of North Carolina and Chesapeake Bay. In support of his convictions, he financed three expeditions to the area. While these were being made, Raleigh himself took part in the war against Spain, and he was largely responsible for the success of the attack against Cadiz.

The first expedition, in 1584, was a reconnaisance trip, but the next year more than a hundred settlers were put ashore at Wokoken. They established a base, but there were so many quarrels and clashes with the Indians, that they had to be rescued by Sir Francis Drake in 1586.

The next year there was another attempt at a genuine settlement. Families were induced to emigrate by the promise of land. Farming and trade with the Indians were also planned. Because of financial difficulties in England, and the threat of the Spanish Armada, no relief ship was sent until 1589. When if finally arrived, no trace of the settlers was found, and the fate of the "lost colony of Roanoke" has remained a mystery to this day.

Since the Queen could not bear to be parted from Raleigh, he had to content himself with supplying the largest ship, the *Raleigh,* and some two thousand pounds in money for the expeditions. The object of the venture was to explore the coast of Florida, but actually the expedition took possession of the area now know as Virginia. Ever the perfect courtier, Raleigh suggested that the region be named after Her Majesty. This gallantry brought its immediate reward, for after he was knighted, the inscription, "Lord and Governor of Virginia" was added to his coat-of-arms.

In his thinking, Raleigh was far in advance of his time, because he foresaw that England must look to the West instead of the East for her economic survival. Hence his backing of the idea to start colonies in America. Although he is given credit for founding the state of Virginia, and the capital of North Carolina is named after him, Sir Walter Raleigh never actually set foot in North America.

In 1595, however, Raleigh sailed on a six months' voyage of exploration to the coast of South America and made extensive explorations of what is now New Guinea. When he returned to England he wrote that brilliant narrative of adventure, *The Discoverie of Guiana.*

In 1590, the Queen gave Raleigh a Dorset manor called Sherborne, which he had long wanted to own. Dating from the early twelfth century, the castle had fallen into disrepair, so Raleigh built himself a Tudor mansion near by, parts of which are incorporated in Major Digby's stately dwelling.

The Raleigh coat-of-arms in a window of the room where he was born.

Sherborne Manor was nineteen miles north of Dorchester.

Despite his successes, Raleigh was rapidly losing favor at Court. He had become involved with one of the Queen's ladies-in-waiting, Bess Throckmorton. When the Queen found out about this involvement she put Raleigh in the Tower of London for most of the year 1592. Raleigh had committed the unpardonable crime, in Elizabeth's eyes, of marriage. When he was released, Raleigh and his bride went to Sherborne to live, and there their sons were born.

Essex had begun to replace Raleigh in the Queen's favors, and from this time on, his fortunes at Court declined. When James I succeeded Elizabeth in 1603, he had Raleigh locked in the Tower a second time. The alleged offense was treason, although it is unlikely that he was involved in a plot to put Arabella Stuart on the throne (in place of James I). After a long and complex trial, in which Raleigh conducted his own eloquent defense, he was sentenced to death. Only when he

The Church of All Saints, where the Raleigh family worshipped.

was actually upon the scaffold was the sentence commuted to one of life imprisonment.

The people respected and worshipped him. Crowds flocked to the walls of the Tower in the hope of catching sight of him as he took his daily walk. When he appeared, the crowd waved and cheered, and Raleigh would turn to face them and bow gravely. Many distinguished admirers called upon him in the Tower—ambassadors and courtiers, noblemen and rich merchants from the city, and even King James' Danish Queen, Anne, and his intelligent son, Henry, Prince of Wales. "Only my father would keep such a bird in a cage," said young Prince Henry.

James tried to put a stop to the great admiration that was accorded Raleigh, and he dismissed the sympathetic lieutenant who guarded him and put a more severe and embittered man in his place. During the time of the sympathetic guard, Lady Raleigh actually lived in the Bloody Tower with her husband, and their second son Carew was born

there. When she was ejected by the unsympathetic guard, she moved into a house near by on Tower Hill. The King refused him the use of the garden, refused to let Lady Raleigh's coach enter the Tower Gate, and dismissed the black servants whom Raleigh had brought from Guiana. Raleigh's friends were so influential, however, that they prevented his life from becoming too miserable.

Raleigh took his meals in the Lieutenant's Lodgings, a half-timbered building on Tower Green now known as the Queen's House and used as the home of the Resident Governor of the Tower. The ramparts leading to the Lieutenant's Lodgings, along which Raleigh used to walk, are named after him. During his imprisonment, Raleigh performed numerous scientific experiments in a small hut on Tower Green, and he is said to have discovered the principle of distilling fresh water from salt water. The hut was actually a little hen house by the garden wall, which he had converted into a laboratory.

Raleigh received frequent visits from the Prince of Wales and spent many hours discussing history, astronomy, and seamanship with him. He also made ship models and wrote what was intended to be a history of the world. A copy of his history, dated 1676, is shown in the Bloody Tower.

In 1610, Raleigh sought permission to conduct another expedition to the region of the Orinoco, in the northern part of South America, where he hoped to find rich deposits of gold. It was nearly seven years before permission was granted and he finally set sail. Unfortunately, things went wrong from the very beginning—the weather was bad, the ships were disabled, the water ran short, the crews came down with scurvy and fever, and the Spaniards blocked their way to the mine. Raleigh returned to England, then tried to leave Plymouth and escape to France. He was arrested and brought back to the Tower, where he was told that he would be executed in accordance with the sentence for treason that had been passed upon him fifteen years before.

The date of execution was set for October 29, 1618. On the night before his death, the following lines were written by Raleigh in his Bible:

"THE AUTHOR'S EPITAPH, made by himself.
Even such is Time, which takes in trust
Our Youth, and Joys, and all we have,
And pays us but with age and dust,

Which in the dark and silent grave,
When we have wandered all our ways,
Shuts up the story of our days:
And from which Earth, and Grave, and Dust,
The Lord shall raise me up, I trust."

Sir Walter Raleigh faced death without a tremor. On the scaffold, he asked the headsman if he might feel the axe to make sure that it was sharp enough. After touching the edge with his fingers he smiled and turned to the sheriff, "This is a sharp medicine," he said, "but it is a physician for all diseases."

Declining to be blindfolded, he said to the executioner, "When I stretch forth my hands, dispatch me." The headsman was trembling so much that he could not bring himself to strike the blow when the signal was given. After a pause, Raleigh gave the signal a second time, but still the headsman seemed powerless to move.

"What dost thou fear?" called out Raleigh in a strong clear voice. "Strike, man, strike!"

The headsman struck then, but it was a fumbling blow, and the axe had to be raised again. The watching crowd in the old Palace Yard of Westminster remained silent, until a man called out, "We have not another such head to be cut off."

And thus died one of the last of the great Elizabethans.

As was the custom, the head was shown on each side of the scaffold and then put into a red leather bag over which his velvet gown was thrown. It was embalmed and carried to Lady Raleigh in a morning coach. She lived twenty-nine years after her husband's death and carried his head with her, wherever she went. When she died, at the age of eighty-two, the head passed into the care of Raleigh's son, Carew, and is supposed to have been buried with him. Carew Raleigh was buried on January 1, 1667, in his father's grave at St. Margaret's.

After the execution, Raleigh's body was brought to St. Margaret's Church for burial. At the right of the altar in this beautiful twelfth-century church there is a bronze plaque that states: "Within the chancel of this church was interred the body of the great Sir Walter Raleigh, K.T. on the day he was beheaded in Old Palace Yard, Westminster. October 29. An. Dom. 1618" There is also his coat-of-arms, set in an elaborate stone scroll, with the admonition:

The entrance to the Tower of London.

"Reader should you reflect on his errors
Remember his many virtues
And that he was a mortal."

There is a magnificent memorial window to Sir Walter Raleigh above the entrance to St. Margaret's Church, given by Americans in 1882. St. Margaret's is next to Westminster Abbey and has long been the parish church of Westminster. The window carries an inscription by James Russell Lowell, as follows:

The New World's sons from England's breast we drew
    Such milk as bids remember whence we came;
Proud of her Past, from which her Present grew,
    This window we inscribe with Raleigh's name."

It was due to Raleigh's initiative that the first attempts were made to "found a new and greater England beyond the seas." He spent a great amount of time and money in his various efforts to found a colony in Virginia, but they were abortive

The moat and drawbridge of the Tower of London.

in the main, because he was not allowed to conduct them in person. The Virgin Queen preferred to have his fine figure and handsome face about her Court.

Raleigh's death retrieved his reputation. As the last of the great Elizabethans and as the dignified martyr of James I's resentment, he became a legend, and the characteristics which made him unpopular in his lifetime were forgotten. In 1829, the works of Sir Walter Raleigh were published in eight volumes.

Unlike many historical characters, Raleigh's place in history grows with the years. He is gradually assuming his proper place as the outstanding soldier, sailor, historian, colonizer, and first imperialist of the British Empire. He was engaged, with many others, in putting England on the map, a map which had hitherto been largely Spanish. Without Raleigh and his fellow adventurers, England might well have become a dependancy of one of the greater European powers of the sixteenth century.

In 1958, there was considerable discussion in the House of Commons about the proposal to place a new statue of Sir Walter Raleigh outside the National Gallery in place of one of James II. The Raleigh statue was commissioned by friends of the English Speaking Union to mark the 350th anniversary of the founding of Jamestown, Virginia. It was finally decided in the House of Lords that the statue should be placed in the garden to be laid out on the frontage of the new Government Offices at Whitehall.

2

John Smith, Pocahontas and John Rolfe

Spurred on by Sir Walter Raleigh's advice and enthusiasm for the project, Queen Elizabeth enlisted the support of many aristocrats in backing the efforts at exploration and colonization in Virginia. Of the one hundred persons who took part in the expedition which resulted in the founding of Jamestown, fifty-four belonged to the rank of gentlemen, while of the hundred and thirty emigrants who reached Jamestown two years later, in 1608, at least thirty-three were gentlemen.

Nothing is known of Captain John Smith's rank or ancestry beyond the fact that he was the son of George and Alice Smith, probably of good yeoman stock. The grit and grip he displayed, as well as his polished manners, gave evidence that he came from first-rate stock. He attributes what he was as a man and soldier to his study of Marcus Aurelius and Machiaevelli's *The Art of War*. Regardless of rank, there were few men of Smith's calibre among the early colonists of Virginia.

John Smith was one of the first company of English colonists to make a successful settlement in America. He was born at Willoughby, Lincolnshire, on January 9, 1580, where his father worked as a farm tenant for Lord Willoughby. Not much is known of his early years except that he attended the Grammar School at Alford and always wanted to go to sea. When his father died, in 1596, young Smith went as a page with the sons of an English nobleman on a tour of the Continent. Young Smith soon left the Willoughby boys, however, and enlisted in a Protestant company in France and fought against the Spaniards, later joining the insurgents in The Netherlands.

For several years, he had some incredible adventures. In the course of these adventures, he had occasion to cross swords with several Turks, who had challenged him. In each case, he succeeded in defeating and then beheading them. As a result, the Prince of Transylvania granted Smith a coat-of-arms bearing three Turks' heads on a shield, with the motto, "Vincere est vivere" — to conquer is to live. This was duly recorded at the Heralds' College, in London, the official register of grants of arms.

About 1606, Smith returned to his home in Lincolnshire and lived a Robinson Crusoe sort of life in the woods. Tiring of that, he took to a life of wandering and fighting, with wonderful adventures in Syria, Turkey, and Morocco. After seeing so much of the Old World, Smith decided to see the New, so he sailed with the expedition to colonize Virginia, which left Blackwall on December 19, 1606.

Trouble broke out before the three ships reached their destination, and Smith was arrested. Some accounts say that he was condemned to be hanged on the charge of wishing to murder the commander of the expedition and set himself up as king of Virginia. A kindly fate spared him, however, and he became one of the most active and useful members of the colony. There he conducted explorations, made important discoveries, and obtained supplies of food from the natives when other sources failed. Of the entire company of settlers, Smith proved to be the most useful, and eventually he was entrusted with the guidance of the colony.

Pocahontas.

During the winter of 1608-09, the colony almost perished for want of food, and half of the hundred and twenty colonists actually died of starvation. Most of Smith's energy was spent in getting corn from the Indians. His courage and ability to get what he wanted from the red men probably saved the colony from destruction. Pocahontas also helped to supply the colonists with corn. She and her train of women carried heavily laden baskets from her father's village to Jamestown, a distance of fifteen miles. There is little doubt that all would have perished had it not been for her devotion to the colony and to John Smith in particular.

When King James ordered John Smith to crown Chief Powhatan, whom the English monarch considered as his new ally, Smith considered it a ridiculous command, but he was forced to obey. When Powhatan was notified of the great honor to be conferred upon him, he suspected a trick and refused to come to Jamestown for the coronation. So Smith had to take the trappings for the ceremony, including a chair of state, a scarlet robe, and the crown, to Powhatan's home. The colonists also took presents for the Indians, including a bed, a basin, and a ewer. Powhatan refused to put on the robe until he was sure there was nothing dangerous about it, and he also balked at kneeling to receive the crown, feeling that it was beneath his dignity to kneel. He was finally persuaded to stoop a little, and once the crown was placed on his head, he was very pleased and gave the Englishmen a raccoon coat as a present for the King of England.

The colony was unable to support itself, however, and the shipments of provisions from England were slow in coming and those that did arrive were far from adequate. Game and fish were abundant, but hard to secure, for, as Smith wrote, "Though there be fish in the sea, fowls in the air, and beasts in the wood, their bounds are so large, they so wild, and we so weak and ignorant that we cannot much trouble them."

In 1609, Smith was badly injured in an explosion and forced to return to England to secure proper treatment. In 1614, he was sent to New England by a group of London merchants. Here, he explored the coast, made a good map of the area, and brought back a valuable cargo of fish and furs.

In 1615, Smith went on another voyage of settlement, this time under the auspices of the Plymouth Company and bearing the title of "Admiral of New England." On this trip, however,

One of his companions has put it on record that "in all his proceedings he (Smith) made justice his first guide and experience his second, ever hating sloth, baseness, pride, and indignity more than any dangers; never allowing himself more than his soldiers; that upon no danger would he send them where he would not lead himself; that he would never see them want what he had or by any means could get them; that he would rather want than borrow, or starve than not pay; that he loved action more than words, and hated falsehood worse than death."

For a time, Smith was the prisoner of the Indians and would have been killed by them had it not been for the timely intervention of Pocahontas, the young daughter of Powhatan, the Indian chief. Apparently the young Indian princess had fallen desperately in love with John Smith and though he was always kind and courteous to her, he did not return her affection in the same way and was not interested in marrying the lovely Indian princess.

his luck ran out and Smith was captured first by pirates and then by the French. He managed to get back to England and stayed there the rest of his life, spending his time writing a number of books about his experiences in the New World.

After Smith left Virginia in 1609, nothing was seen of Pocahontas in Jamestown for three years, until she was brought there as a prisoner in 1612. She had left her father's tribe and was staying with the Potomac Indians, when Captain Argall found her. By bribing the chief to aid him, he persuaded her to go aboard his ship. It was Argall's scheme to hold Pocahontas as a hostage until Powhatan, whose men were still on the warpath, would come to terms.

With her attractive personality and lively intelligence, Pocahontas soon won many friends among the colonists. John Rolfe, one of the colony's outstanding members, fell in love with her. He persuaded the Indian Princess to adopt the Christian faith and she was baptized with the Biblical name of Rebecca. In April of 1614, they were married in the little church at Jamestown, with the High Marshal of Virginia, Sir Thomas Dale, and other colonists and a small group of Indians attending the ceremony.

Pocahontas had married with the full consent of her father. Apparently influenced by his daughter, he now stopped harrassing the colonists and there was peace until his death in 1622. At that time, his brother, Opekankano, long an enemy of the white men, led the terrible massacre of Jamestown. Thus Pocahontas played an important role in bringing peace between the red men and the white settlers.

John Rolfe took his bride to England in 1616, where she was received as a princess and presented at Court. Pocahontas soon became the rage of London society. Her portrait was engraved by the great artist, Simon van Pass, and an inscription on it gives her age as twenty-one. One can see in this portrait the magnificent eyes and handsome face, but the high white ruff and tall stilted hat seem out of place for this lovely creature from the wild Virginia forest.

In order to get some first-hand facts about England, old Powhatan had sent an Indian chieftain with Pocahontas' party. Instructed to find out how many people there were in the country, the agent began cutting notches in a big stick, but soon became weary of the task. Upon his return to Virginia, he replied to Powhatan, "Count

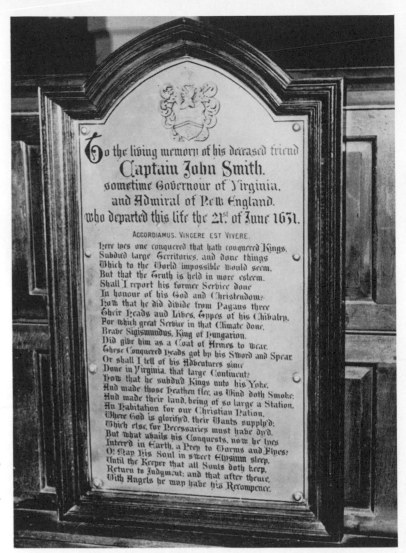

The plaque honoring John Smith that hangs in the Church of the Holy Sepulchre, London.

the stars in the sky, the leaves on the trees, and the sands upon the seashore, such is the number of people in England."

When John Smith learned that Pocahontas was in England, he at once went to see her at Brentford, where she was staying. She was so overcome with emotion on seeing him, that she could not speak, but turned and hid her face. When he returned a short time later, she said, "They did always tell us you were dead and I knew not otherwise until I came to Plymouth."

No doubt Smith was also deeply affected by this meeting with Pocahontas, for he wrote about it at once to Queen Anne, wife of James I. After telling how Pocahontas saved his life, he said: "She hazarded the beating out of her own brains in order to save mine, and not only that, but she prevailed with her father that I was safely conducted to Jamestown, where I found about eight

The plaque honoring Pocahontas that hangs in St. George's Church, Gravesend, England.

This letter to the Queen of England was an eloquent tribute to Pocahontas and proof of the place that she held in a gallant heart.

Pocahontas' beauty and the devotion she had shown to the English settlers made her very popular, and she was received with enthusiasm. She was hailed as the daughter of an American "king," and feted and acclaimed as such. Pocahontas and John Rolfe had one son, Thomas, who lived for many years in England and then emigrated to Virginia. Many prominent Virginia families trace their descent from this first Anglo-American marriage.

John Smith never married. He made no more voyages, his days of adventure were over. His last days were spent in making maps and writing his books. His *General History of Virginia* was published in 1624 and his *True Travels* in 1629. He died on June 21, 1631, at the home of his friend Sir Samuel Saltonstall, at the age of fifty-one. It was not until 1907 that a monument was erected to Captain John Smith at Jamestown.

Unfortunately, the damp English climate did not agree with the Indian princess, and Pocahontas died in March, 1617, at Gravesend. Her body was laid to rest at St. George's Church, in Gravesend, and her death was recorded in the parish records. A beautiful statue of Pocahontas — the first native-born American to marry a native-born Englishman — stands in the churchyard in front of St. George's Church.

After the death of his wife, John Rolfe returned to Virginia, in 1617, where he was colonial secretary and recorder and later a member of the council of state. It is thought that he was killed in an Indian massacre... Their son, Thomas Rolfe, was left with an uncle in England, where he remained until he was grown. Then he went to his mother's country and became the ancestor of some of Virginia's first families.

In the church at Heacham, Norfolk, which was John Rolfe's birthplace, there is a memorial tablet to Rolfe and his wife Pocahontas, the "Nonpareil of Virginia."

In London, deep within the "City," at the corner of Holborn Viaduct and Giltspur Street, there is a church that should be known to every American visitor. Originally built in the fifteenth century, this Church of the Holy Sepulchre was restored in 1950. Its special interest for Americans, however, lies in the fact that Captain John Smith

and thirty miserable, poor creatures, to keep possession of all those large territories of Virginia. Such was the weakness of the poor commonwealth that, had the savages not fed us, we directly had starved...and this relief, most gracious Queen, was commonly brought us by the lady Pocahontas. When her father sought to surprise me, having but eighteen men with me, the dark night could not affright her from coming through the irksome woods and with watered eyes give me intelligence, with her best advice to escape from his fury, which had he known, he surely would have slain her... During the time of two or three years she, next to God, was still the instrument to preserve this colony from death, famine, and utter confusion, which if in those times had once been dissolved, Virginia might have lain as it was at our first arrival to this day."

tatue of Pocahontas in the churchyard of St. George's Church, avesend, England.

General view of the churchyard in Gravesend, England.

was buried here. The exact position of his tomb is not known, but the brass plate in the church is a copy of the one which originally marked his grave.

The memorial window to John Smith was designed by Francis Skeat and was presented in 1968 by the late Bradford Smith, biographer of John Smith. The window shows the great Captain surrounded by nautical instruments, carrying a copy of his famous map of Virginia. On each side are the two men who gave him so much help and encouragement, Robert Bertie and Sir Samuel Saltonstall. It was Saltonstall who bore the costs of printing Smith's *Sea Grammar*. He also held open house for Smith at his home in Snow Hill, to the west of the Church. In this house a room was reserved for Smith, who kept a trunk there, containing his personal books and belongings. Sir Samuel's first cousin, Sir Richard Saltonstall, founded the Massachusetts branch of the family

which continues to this day. High at the top of the memorial window are the letters "S H," which stand for St. Helen's, the church in Willoughby where John Smith was baptized on January 9, 1580. Above are the coats-of-arms of the three men — Smith, Bertie, and Saltonstall — and other friends and patrons. Under Smith's feet is the seal of the Virginia Company, and below are the three little ships in which the pioneers crossed the Atlantic.

There is a memorial plaque to Pocahontas in the Church of the Holy Sepulchre. The large brass memorial plaque to John Smith has a lengthy inscription which begins: "To the living memory of his deceased friend, Captain John Smith, sometime Governor of Virginia and Admiral of New England, who departed this life the 21st of June, 1631." This is followed by a lengthy description of Captain Smith's life and work.

Throughout the church, the kneeling pads, or "kneelers," have been covered with beautiful embroidery, done by dedicated and skilled needle-pointers throughout the world, portraying the history and associations of the Church. One such kneeler shows John Smith's coat-of-arms, and another represents the map drawn by John Smith of the land owned by Powhatan, father of Pocahontas. This map, incidentally, formed the basis of his later famous map of Virginia. Another kneeler of special interest to Americans is that showing two flags, that of England and the first Union flag, to define the passing of land from Colony to Statehood, 1606-1777. The kneeler for the priest's chair carries a simple Jerusalem Cross, symbolic of the Church of the Holy Sepulchre in Jerusalem, from which this Church takes its name.

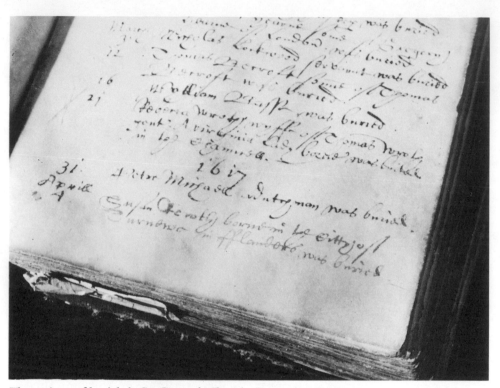

The register of burials in St. George's Church, Gravesend, England.

3
The Pilgrims

It is interesting to note how "English" was the first colonization of Virginia and New England. In the early annals, comparatively few Scots' names appear and rarely an Irish one. In the early days of migration it was from the countries of northern and eastern England, notably Yorkshire, Nottinghamshire, and Lincolnshire, that most of the colonists came. The Pilgrims, in particular their two great leaders, William Bradford and William Brewster, came from neighboring villages: Scrooby, in Nottinghamshire, and Austerfield, just across the border in Yorkshire. It was these two men, Bradford and Brewster, who supplied the courage, the ideals, and the perseverance that led to the fateful voyage of the *Mayflower* and the establishing of civil government in the colony they founded.

Scrooby and Austerfield are an easy drive from the cathedral city of York, and are well worth a visit. Trains from London to York are frequent and the three-hour ride is very pleasant. Once in York, it is easy to hire a taxi or rent a car and go directly to the scene. The villages are too small to have a restaurant or hotel, but they are not far from the town of Bawtry, where meals and rooms are available at an old coaching inn called The Crown. Scrooby, however, does have a pub, fittingly named the Pilgrim Fathers, prominently located on the old Great North Road.

It is thought that the project for the colonization of New England was first discussed in the village of Scrooby, thus making it, in essence, the germinal point of the present United States. There can be no question that at Scrooby the spirit arose which led to the founding of the first colony in New England. In 1955, 335 years after the historic sailing of the *Mayflower*, 152 members of the Society of Mayflower Descendants came from America to visit the historic villages of Scrooby and Austerfield. In each place, they erected an appropriate tablet in the parish church. In St. Helena's, the tablet in honor of William Bradford describes him as "the first American citizen of the English race who bore rule by the free choice of his brethren."

Austerfield and Scrooby are still unspoiled and in many ways untouched by modern civilization. As the birthplace of the beliefs that led to the founding of America, they will always be dear to the hearts of Americans.

William Brewster, one of the chief founders of the Plymouth Colony, was born in Scrooby in late 1566 or early 1567. His father, also named William, was bailiff of the manor of Scrooby, which belonged to the Archbishop of York, who used it as a residence when making his rounds of the diocese. Today, only the farmhouse and outbuildings remain of the original palatial manor house. Many royal and noble personages stayed at this manor, whose history goes back to 1170.

In addition to being bailiff, William Brewster's father was also postmaster, that is, he furnished horses to travelers and was at times required to furnish them with food and lodging. In olden days, Scrooby was one of four posts on the way to Scotland along the Great North Road. It was an official office looking after the traffic and letters to and from London. After the Great Northern

The Crown Hotel in Bawtry, not far from Scrooby, England.

Railway was built, with a station at Scrooby, the village lost its importance as a posting center. Through the centuries it has remained the center of a farming community. The Brewster house is quite near St. Wilfred's Church, and part of the house has been preserved as a museum of the Tudor period.

Today Scrooby has a population of about four hundred, but it has remained a typical English village, with the spire of the parish church shooting up into the blue and seeming to look down with quiet delight on the woodland that once formed part of Sherwood Forest, haunt of legendary Robin Hood.

St. Wilfred's Church, where young Brewster was baptized, is the center of interest for American visitors. The church was named for a monk who became Bishop of York and is said to have built York Minster. It is an ancient embattled edifice of stone in the early English and Decorated styles. It is thought that a church existed on this site since Saxon times, but the present building dates from the fourteenth century and has had several restorations. The steeple, however, has survived the many changes and retains its unique feature: a four-sided tower topped by an eight-sided spire. From a distance, it looks like a sharpened pencil. In 1936, extensive repairs to this steeple were made possible by generous gifts from friends in America. The porch, with its stone roof, has remained unaltered.

The interior, with its carved oak altar and sixteenth-century benches, is of special interest to Americans. The two benches in the chancel and the one near the organ are known as the Brewster Pews. They are also noteworthy for their intricate, running-foliage carving of the ancient Christian symbol of the vine.

In this quiet village, young Brewster grew up. Life was not without its livelier episodes when gay cavalcades of travelers appeared or when some dignitary stopped to see the Archbishop. No doubt young William heard many stirring tales about the world beyond the seas, for those were the days of Drake and Raleigh, of Cabot and Frobisher.

The Pilgrim Fathers Pub, in Scrooby, England.

St. Helena's Church in Austerfield.

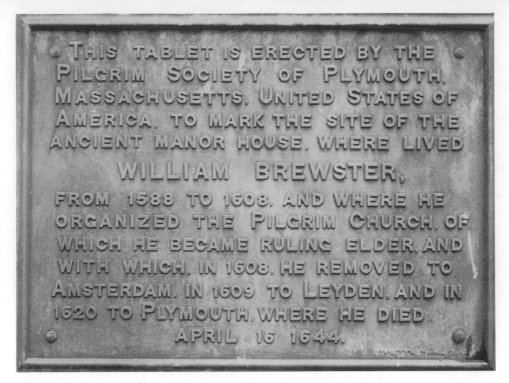

The plaque on Brewster's house, in Scrooby.

Young Brewster matriculated at Cambridge on December 3, 1580, at the age of fourteen. It is not known how long he remained there, although Bradford, in his *Memoir,* says that "Brewster spent some small time there, attaining some knowledge of the Latin tongue and some insight in the Greek." He did not take a degree, but while in his teens entered the service of William Davison, Secretary of State to Queen Elizabeth. Davison found young Brewster "discreet and faithful" and "esteemed him as a son rather than as a servant," employed him in matters of special trust and confidence, in preference to the other clerks.

In August, 1585, Brewster went with Davison to The Netherlands, where he saw a brave people fighting for their national and religious freedom. These months in Holland undoubtedly had a powerful influence on Brewster, awakening feelings and trains of thought that he never forgot. Brewster continued to serve Davison until his downfall in 1587. At this time Brewster turned away from the dangerous attractions of the Court and returned to Scrooby, where he acted as assistant to his father in the duties of the post.

In 1590, after the death of his father, Brewster succeeded to the tenancy of the manor farm and applied for his father's position as postmaster. Now living at the manor house, Brewster often entertained a large group of Separatists, who gathered for worship in one of the outbuildings of the manor, there being no other place where they dared hold their meetings.

When Protestantism became the authorized religion for England and took the place of the old religion (Catholicism), it had a political as well as a strictly religious position. If a man denied the Anglican church it meant that he was likely to be disloyal and deny the authority of the king. As King James said, "No bishop, no king." The Puritans, as they were called, wished to "purify" the church from within, acknowledging the King as its head but wishing to rid its worship of details they thought smacked too much of Catholicism. Besides the Puritans, there were other groups known as Separatists who refused to have bishops and were considered therefore disloyal to the King.

Brewster had a good salary and was able to support the young Separatist movement in its early days. Bradford, too, was a man of independent means. A third leader was John Robinson, a non-conformist pastor in the Lincolnshire village of Gainsborough. Robinson was a university graduate and had begun as an orthodox parson. These three, therefore, were well educated men of good social position, and they had enough good sense and organizing ability to attract to themselves a Separatist church at Scrooby, "to worship God in their own manner." Even so, they ran great risks.

William Bradford, the son of William and Alice Hanson Bradford, was born in nearby Austerfield

The farmhouse of the old Manor, in Scrooby.

St. Wilfred's Church, in Scrooby.

The interior of St. Wilfred's Church, in Scroob

in 1589. The family held the rank of yeomen, and on the death of his father in 1591, young Bradford was left with a comfortable inheritance. He was educated by his grandparents and then his uncles, who trained him as a farmer. His attention was turned to religion through the reading of the Geneva Bible at the age of twelve or thirteen. He would walk five miles to the village of Babworth to hear Rev. Clifton, the Puritan rector.

The ancestral Bradford home, Austerfield Manor, is still standing, on the main road to Thorne. It is now the home of Colonel and Mrs. W.F. Bracewell, who in recent years restored it from a somewhat decrepit state.

Bradford was baptized in St. Helena's Church, in Austerfield, on March 19, 1589, according to the church register. The church was named for Helena, the mother of Emperor Constantine, who introduced Christianity into the Roman Empire. St. Helena made a pilgrimage to the Holy Land in her old age and superintended excavations in Calvary.

St. Helena's is one of the best existing examples of the small Norman church. Originally built in 1080, the church has been renovated many times, but a great part of the existing stone work of the nave and the beautiful chancel arch are part of the original church and date from shortly after the Norman Conquest.

Bradford soon threw in his lot with the rest, in spite of the strong opposition of his relatives and the scoffing of his neighbors. He joined the Separatists on May 1, 1606, at the home of his friend Brewster. Being a youth of spirit and resolution, as well as means, his cooperation no doubt tended to strengthen and encourage the little group, whose progress thus far had been due largely to the zeal and influence of Brewster. As regards education and experience of the world, Brewster was undoubtedly the best qualified to take the lead.

Another outstanding leader among the Pilgrims was Miles Standish, immortalized in Longfellow's poem, "The Courtship of Miles Standish." He was born at Duxbury Hall, between Wigan and Chorley,

The plaque in St. Wilfred's Church.

ST. WILFRED'S CHURCH, SCROOBY, NOTTINGHAMSHIRE, ENGLAND, WHERE WILLIAM BREWSTER WAS BAPTIZED (C.1566). HE BECAME A SEPARATIST, AND WAS THE ELDER AND SPIRITUAL LEADER OF THE PILGRIMS IN PLYMOUTH, NEW ENGLAND, UNTIL HIS DEATH IN 1643-44. THE GENERAL SOCIETY OF MAYFLOWER DESCENDANTS (U.S.A. 1897) WALDO MORGAN ALLEN GOVERNOR GENERAL ON THEIR FIRST PILGRIMAGE - 152, BY PLANES - TO THE NETHERLANDS AND ENGLAND SEPTEMBER 22 - OCTOBER 6, 1955 335 YEARS AFTER THE SAILING OF THE MAYFLOWER

in Lancashire. The coat-of-arms of his family, showing an owl with a rat in its claw, may be seen in the chancel window of the old church at Chorley, where the quaint family pew of the Standish family stands in the nave opposite the pulpit. When he settled in New England, Standish gave the name Duxbury to his new estate. Little is known of Miles Standish's early life, however, except that he was a soldier to his finger tips. Standish joined the Pilgrims in Leyden in 1609 and became one of the company that sailed in 1620. Before the group had disembarked, Miles Standish had been appointed military commander. His duty was to gather a small body of armed men and to explore the country around to make sure that no lurking foes were about. On November 21, sixteen such warriors under the command of Captain Miles Standish were despatched ashore on a second exploration.

Five years later, Standish revisited England as agent for the colony and brought back supplies the following year. Returning as the "first commissioned military officer of New England," Miles Standish settled down for the remainder of his days at Duxbury, living thirty years in his new home, leaving behind a reputation that has inspired many poets, one of whom called him "the Greatheart of the Pilgrim band."

Another early settler, much like Standish in character, was John Winthrop, who became the first governor of the Massachusetts Bay Colony. Born at Edwardston, Suffolk, in January, 1587, Winthrop's early life was spent at Groton Manor, five miles east of Sudbury. He was admitted to Trinity College, Cambridge, in December, 1602, and continued there until his marriage in 1605. His sympathy with the Separatist movement caused him to think of emigrating. When the London proprietors of the Massachusetts Company decided to transfer the seat of government to the New World, they sent John Winthrop as governor. He went to New England in 1630 with eleven ships and a large number of emigrants, arriving at Salem in June. The following year he and his fellow colonists moved to the site that is now Boston, which they founded. For twelve years, John Winthrop was governor of the colony, and he exerted a positive influence, with his kindly disposition, and his frugal, temperate, and industrious habits.

Brewster's pew in St. Wilfred's Church.

At Groton, near Sudbury, Suffolk, there are many memorials to Governor Winthrop and his family. The church contains tablets to the memory of the Governor and his first wife, Mary Forth, and to his second wife, Thomasina Clopton. Windows in the nave and aisles contain shields bearing the coat-of-arms of both these families. Adam Winthrop, grandfather of John, was buried in the churchyard, where his tomb bears the coat-of-arms of the family.

After James I came to the throne, the threats of persecution forced the little group of Separatists to flee England and seek refuge abroad. They went to Boston, a port forty miles east of Scrooby, and negotiated with a Dutch captain to take them to Holland. But the King had closed the ports against all those who had no license to depart, and the

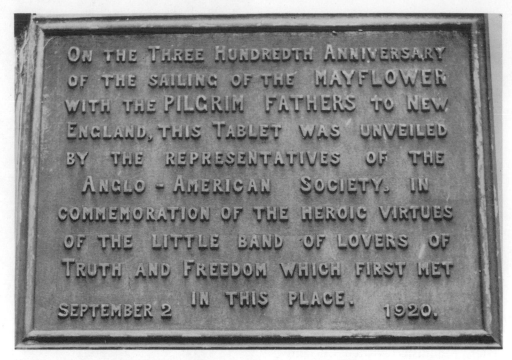

The Mayflower plaque at the old Manor farm.

Dutch captain betrayed them to the authorities. The Pilgrims were hauled ashore, robbed, and barbarously treated. After languishing in prison for a month, they were dismissed, but Brewster, Bradford, and five other leaders were kept longer in prison and forced to pay heavy fines.

Thanks to the kindliness and humanity of the magistrates of Boston, the fugitives were treated with courtesy; in fact, they would have been discharged if that course had been within the magistrates' power. This kindness must have left a lasting impression, for in later years the fugitives named their chief city in America after the English port where they had been imprisoned. The English port of Boston was noted at the time for its liberality and non-conformity, as well as for sending out many notable men to the New England colony. Among the emigrants from Boston were the vicar, John Cotton; three governors, Thomas Dudley, Bellingham, and Leverett; and the magistrate William Coddington, who later became governor of Rhode Island.

The following spring, however, the group of determined Pilgrims found another Dutch vessel, this time in Hull, which took them to Holland. Although this country was noted for its tolerance regarding religious matters, the group from England had to learn new trades and handicrafts in order to make a living. After seven months in Amsterdam, they moved to Leyden. From 1609 to 1620, the group in Leyden held their own church services in the home of their pastor, John Robinson.

They had been English farmers, but now they had to work in textile industries. William Bradford became a weaver. When they saw their children taking up new ways and learning a new language, they were afraid of losing their English identity in a foreign land. Their life in Holland was no bed of roses, and the idea of "living as English folk under English rule" which had first been discussed at Scrooby, came up again, strongly supported by both Brewster and Bradford.

Brewster had set up a printing shop in order to bring out such theological works as could not be safely published in England. When some of these found their way to London, the English government, in 1610, asked to have Brewster arrested and sent to England for trial. At that particular time the Dutch had special reasons for wanting to be on good terms with King James, so they agreed. In due course, someone with a name not unlike Brewster was arrested. When Brewster heard this he returned to London and found a safe and commodious hiding place. With the aid of friends, he was able to make plans for the emigration scheme.

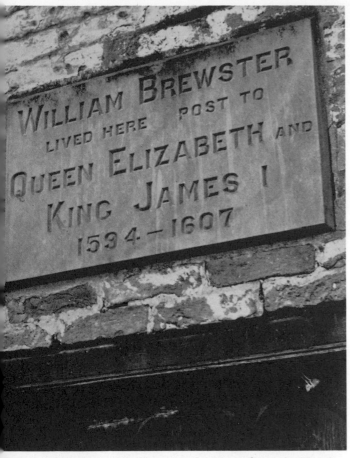

The plaque at the Manor house in Scrooby.

Originally, the choice of the Pilgrims lay between Guiana and Virginia, but for obvious reasons the latter was finally chosen. When Brewster was working for Davison, one of his companions was Sir Edwin Sandys, the son of the Archbishop of York and afterwards treasurer of the Virginia Company. With Sandys' assistance, a patent (grant) was applied for and obtained for a tract of land to found a settlement in the colony of Virginia.

In 1620, a man named Weston, an ironmonger with some capital, appeared and made a proposal for a joint stock company, which would be one of many such companies formed in this period by a loosely knit group of London investors calling themselves Merchant Adventurers. As the Leyden group was getting poorer every day, Weston's solution seemed providential.

It was a hard contract that the Pilgrims signed. For the first seven years they would be almost slaves, since most of their revenue would revert to the Merchant Adventurers. In many cases they had to leave members of their families behind. Mary Brewster left her husband, still in hiding, and three of her five children; the Bradfords left their five-year-old son behind, for his greater safety. Others left their children or their wives behind, and

The Bradford house in Austerfield.

Groton Church, near Sudbury, Suffolk, containing memorials the Winthrop family.

came across the Sound. The only habitation in view was the residence of the Governor of Plymouth Fort, rising above the walls of the fort on the eastern end of the Hoe. It had been built only twenty-five years before, at the insistence of Sir Francis Drake.

The evening before they sailed, the Pilgrims had an open-air prayer meeting on a grassy slope overlooking Plymouth Harbor. On the morning of September 16, one hundred and four passengers and crew boarded the *Mayflower,* while many others were left behind. This double-decked, three-masted English merchant ship was very small for so many people. It was about ninety feet long and twenty-five feet wide, and displaced not more than 180 tons. She had a wooden forecastle for the crew, a wooden sterncastle for the officers and captain, where a few of the more important passengers were allowed to sleep, and a main deck where the rest were packed in without bunks or hammocks. The ship's longboat was used for

it was to be years before these families were united once more.

On July 31, 1620, sixteen men, eleven women, and nineteen children gathered at the dockside of Delftshaven in Holland and went aboard the *Speedwell,* a boat of some sixty tons bound for Southampton in England. There they were to meet another party and make with them the adventurous voyage to the New World. The *Speedwell* was in bad shape, so they had to put in at Dartmouth harbor for repairs. Here they stayed ten days, while the ship was being repaired.

Finally the *Speedwell* reached Southampton, where she joined her sister ship, the *Mayflower.* On August 15, the two ships left Southampton, but the *Speedwell* was still having trouble, and the captain refused to attempt the trip across the Atlantic. The two ships put in at Plymouth, where they stayed a few days. The passengers may well have wondered where the town could be as they

The interior of Groton Church, near Sudbury.

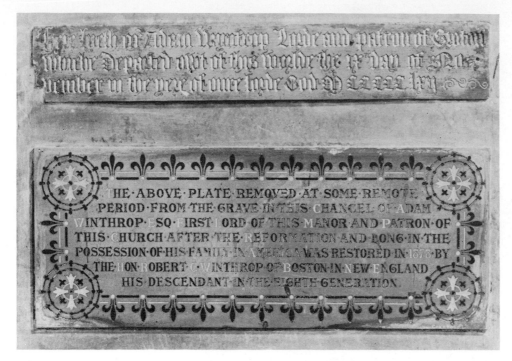

The plaque to Adam Winthrop, in Groton Church.

sleeping by some of the Pilgrims and had to be repaired later. In bad weather, rain and salt water leaked through from the upper deck, which had a flimsy covering of canvas. Only one thing could be said in favor of the *Mayflower,* she had a sweet smell from her use in the wine trade, whereas other ships had developed a foul stench from their cargoes of whales and other animals.

For sixty-seven days men, women, and children were crowded together, in storm and fine weather, making for an unknown shore. One of the main beams amidships was cracked in a storm and the master and his officers considered turning back, but fortunately a passenger had the special tool necessary for making the repairs and so, as William Bradford recorded in his diary, they "committed themselves to the will of God and resolved to proceed."

Often the winds were so violent and contrary that they had to drift for whole days. A young man was swept overboard by one wave and back again by the next. One man died and one baby was born, and named Oceanus. A second baby was born when they were anchored at the end of the voyage and called Peregrine (the Pilgrim). He was the first Englishman to be born in New England and lived to be eighty-three.

Of the sixty-six men, twenty-six women, and twelve children, only fifty-three, just more than half, survived the first year in the New World. When Captain Jones and his crew insisted on sailing the *Mayflower* back to England the following spring, not a single one of the Pilgrims asked to return. These fifty Pilgrims were to become the ancestors of nearly a million Americans today.

William Bradford became governor of Plymouth Colony in April, 1621, and, excepting for a five-year period, was governor until his death in 1657. He wrote a history of Plymouth, which was found in 1855 in Fulham Palace Library, in England. In 1898, the then Archbishop of Canterbury presented this manuscript to the

The tomb of Adam Winthrop, grandfather of John, in the churchyard of Groton Church.

The memorial window to the Winthrop family, in Groton Church.

American nation. A copy of the scroll recording the thanks of the Society of Mayflower Descendants is to be found in the vestry of the Church of St. Helena, in Austerfield.

Perhaps there has never been another small group who have shown themselves so willing to endure hardships for the sake of the religion they wished to practice. Certainly their toughness endured when many other adventurers, interested chiefly in gold, slaves, or other riches, were wiped out or forced to return home. And it all started in two small, insignificant villages — Scrooby and Austerfield — that most of the world has never heard of.

The *Mayflower* memorial at Southampton.

4

Plymouth and the *Mayflower*

To all American patriots, Plymouth, England, is an all but holy spot, with a wealth of mementos regarding the Pilgrims, as well as those earlier adventurers, Drake and Raleigh. Since it is a three-and-a-half hour train ride from London, and since there is so much to see, visitors should plan to stay overnight.

The history of Plymouth stretches back over 900 years to the time of William the Conqueror, when it was a small settlement known as Sutton Harbor. Sutton, in turn, had been a port ever since the days of the Saxons and the Normans. For hundreds of years there had been nets drying on its quays, fishermen hawking their catch around the town, and sailors quenching their thirst at the pubs and the Mitre Inn.

Thus in the days of the Pilgrims, more than 350 years ago, Plymouth was already an old town, having been incorporated before 1439, when its first Guildhall was built. In 1606 the original Guildhall was torn down and a new one erected.

The market, with its fresh fish and other foods, was held at street level under the granite arches and columns which held up the Guildhall. At one end of the building was the debtors' prison, with a place where criminals were confined. In the castle on the hill, with its huge tower at each corner, Catherine of Aragon had spent her first nights in England when she came to be Henry VIII's unhappy bride.

Because of the strategic importance of Sutton Harbor, which commands the entrance to the English Channel, Plymouth grew to become one of the chief ports of the realm during the reign of Elizabeth I. This was a Golden Age for Plymouth, with expeditions setting forth for Newfoundland, Virginia, and Bermuda. In those far-off days, Plymouth was bursting at the seams. Money, ships, merchants, sea captains, foreign privateers, swaggering adventurers, and the rich prizes of Africa, South America, and the Spanish Main were pouring into the town. These were the men building a new world, with its wealth creating a new Britain. Not only economically, but culturally as well, England was flowering, for it was the age of Shakespeare and Bacon, of Ben Jonson and Milton.

It must have been a powerful force, indeed, that would cause men to leave the land of their birth at such a time and risk the perils of the sea to seek a new home in an unknown and untried land. Only man's inborn desire for freedom could motivate men under these circumstances.

In 1970, during the reign of a second Elizabeth, descendants of those valiant Pilgrims and thousands of other Americans visited Plymouth on the 350th anniversary of the sailing of the *Mayflower*. There are now only the crumbling remains of the old castle that had four towers, but there are a number of the old homes and inns and taverns. One can walk on the old wharf and see the actual steps on which the Pilgrims descended to board the *Mayflower* for their historic sailing. It doesn't matter that a century and a half after the sailing, the Pilgrims' descendants fought to free themselves from the mother country. Today the two nations are very close. To paraphrase a nuptial cliché, one might say that "while England lost a colony, it gained an ally."

A young lady wearing the Pilgrim dress of the 1620s.

On a plaque at the entrance to the Island House, where many of the *Mayflower* passengers stayed while waiting for the ship to sail, are the names of the 104 brave souls who sailed to America in 1620.

From existing records, it would seem that the Pilgrims greatly appreciated their stay in Plymouth, because the townspeople themselves were notoriously non-conformist and showed great sympathy for the courageous "separatists" who sought asylum on foreign shores. Also, many of the Plymouth men had sailed to the New World and had traded and fished off the coast of North America. No doubt they gave the Pilgrims invaluable advice, unobtainable elsewhere, on the problems that would face them.

When the big day came, the 180-ton *Mayflower* took on board 104 passengers, more than thirty of whom were children. All but three of the women were wives. There was also a crew of thirty. It took courage indeed to sail in September,

a month notorious for hurricanes at sea. The little ship was no sooner out of sight of land than the Pilgrims' miseries began. Herded in narrow, cramped quarters, with none of today's medicines or other amenities, the passengers became sick and many of them stayed that way for days. They were made even more wretched by the curses of a profane young seaman. Suddenly this young man became ill and died, the first casualty of the two-month voyage.

On November 9, exactly fifty-five days after setting sail from Plymouth, the Pilgrims sighted land. It was Cape Cod, in the area previously named New England by Captain John Smith. The Pilgrims wished to sail south to the Hudson River, but because of the perilous shoals, roaring breakers, and lessening wind, they had to make for Cape Cod Bay.

On November 11, they cast anchor and were told by Captain Jones to find a landing place with all possible speed. Winter was at hand and he declared he would not stir until they had found a safe harbor. It was later said that Jones was in league with the Dutch, who were about to found the colony which later became New York, and that he had purposely misled the Pilgrims. Whether by design or fate, they had no choice but to settle in New England, where their patent from the London Virginia Company would be of no value.

They had to devise their own government and that same day, November 11, 1620, in the cabin of the *Mayflower* the Pilgrims drew up the compact which was to serve as their constitution. By virtue of this agreement, which assented to majority rule and extended their church unity to civil government, they launched the long schooling in independence which was to prepare America for the republic. There were nine men who did not sign the Mayflower Compact; perhaps they were too ill, for the ordeal of long exposure and inadequate sea diet was already having its effects. Pilgrim wives had no personal rights and were not invited to sign the Compact.

The job now was to find a place to land, so two exploratory trips were made by several men in a small boat. At this time, there were no white settlements this far north. Through storm and snow the men circled inside Cape Cod Bay, finally choosing a protected area on the mainland as the place for disembarking and making their home.

On December 11, 1620, the Pilgrims stepped

The *Mayflower II* in the shipyard at Brixham.

ashore, on the granite boulder which is today celebrated as Plymouth Rock. Mary Chiltern was the first to spring ashore. This rock, originally fifteen feet long and three feet wide, lay with its points to the east, thus forming a natural pier during several hours of low tide. The Indians called the spot Pawtuxit, but the Pilgrim Fathers preferred the name Captain Smith had given it — Plymouth — in grateful memory of the place where they had received so many kindnesses.

The majority decided it was best to settle on the high ground above the rock, where they found cornfields and running brooks. Every morning a group of men went out to cut timber, returning at night to the ship, which was still the Pilgrims' only home.

There were forty-one deaths by the end of March, due to hunger, privation, scurvy, and other diseases. The Pilgrims buried their dead on the bank above Plymouth Rock, sowing grain above the graves to conceal from the Indians how many men they had lost.

On September 22, 1956, a new *Mayflower* was launched from the Stuart Upham shipyards in Brixham, Devon, as a floating memorial to Anglo-American unity. It differs from the original only in the age of its timber and the fact that there is a radio on board. The 58-foot keel was made from a 120-year-old oak tree grown at Totnes, Devon.

Warwick Charlton, a British public relations man, conceived the idea ten years previously, as a gesture of appreciation for American aid during the war. He organized the *Mayflower* project, raised the money, and got the scheme under way. The ship was designed by William A. Baker, an American naval architect, who spent years poring over old records, trying to evolve a design. The original *Mayflower* had been junked four years after its great voyage, and there were no plans extant. He had one ancient model to go on and

Plymouth Rock, in Massachusetts, with its marble canopy.

A sketch of Plymouth Plantation.

pictures of ships that looked like the *Mayflower.* Mr. Baker's plans were turned over to Stuart Upham, whose shipyard has been building wooden ships for a hundred and fifty years. It took nearly a year to build this second *Mayflower,* and the workers used the same tools that were used to build wooden ships three hundred years ago. The wood came from the forests of Devon itself.

On the day of the launching, an appropriate Shipyard Service was held, conducted by the Rev. H.T. Yeomans, Vicar of Brixham. In April, 1957, the new *Mayflower* sailed to America, with Alan Villiers in charge and a crew of twenty, dressed in Puritan costumes. There were no Americans in the crew, because that would not have been historically accurate. Many of the passengers, however, were descendants of the original Mayflower Company. There were about twenty thousand applications for the voyage, but Mr. Villiers limited the number to thirty-five, including the crew.

Four years after the historic sailing from Plymouth, the original *Mayflower* was put up for sale. Farmers were eager to get oak for building purposes, for the English navy had priority on new oak. A Buckinghamshire farmer purchased the ship and used it in building a barn (see Chapter Five).

The Hoe is Plymouth's famous grass-covered "high place," from which generations of her citizens have witnessed the comings and goings of countless ships of almost every description. The imposing statue of Sir Francis Drake stands on the highest point of the Hoe, as if to give the great navigator the best view of the sea.

The Barbican is one of the most historic parts of Plymouth and was built during the sixteenth century when Sutton Harbor was one of the main bases for the English fleet. Untouched by modern developments, this part of Plymouth retains much of its early character, especially along the waterside and in New Street, where timbered Elizabethan houses face each other across its cobbles. The Island House, on the Barbican beside the water, is known for its association with the Pilgrim Fathers. Some of the Pilgrims lodged at the Island House during their stay in Plymouth. The board with their names does not include the names of any women. Nor are there any people listed as coming from Plymouth. The only person from the West country was Francis Eaton, the shipwright, of Bristol. The best known of all Plymouth's landmarks, however, are the plaque and portico which commemorate the departure of the Pilgrims. You can still see the steps down which they went to board the *Mayflower.*

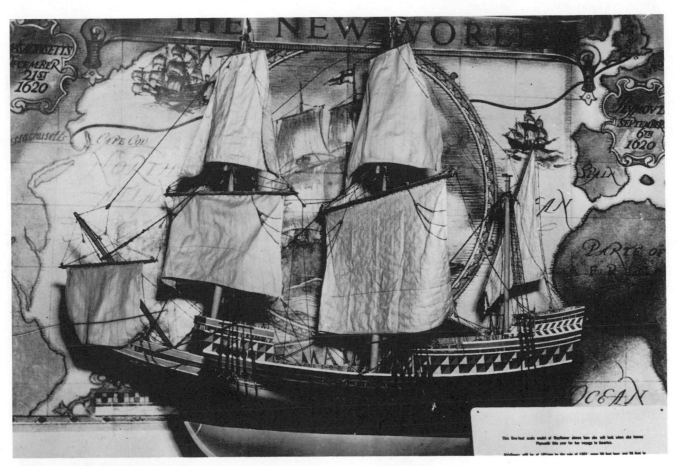

A model of the first *Mayflower.*

Services held at the launching of *Mayflower II*, in 1956.

The building of *Mayflower II*.

In Southampton, too, there is a monument near the quay to commemorate the *Mayflower* and a copper model of the ship is perched on a fifty-foot column. Near by, on the ancient wall next to the West Gate is a plaque which reads: "The Pilgrim Fathers embarked here from the west quay on the *Mayflower,* August 15, 1620."

St. Andrew's Church stands at the top of the Royal Parade in Plymouth. Dating mainly from the fifteenth century, when Plymouth received its charter, it has always been closely associated with the sea and has often been the place of worship for adventurers and pilgrims departing for the New World. Gutted during World War II, St. Andrew's was completely refurbished in the 1950's. An interesting scratching of Drake's crest survived the damage and may be seen on a south wall window-sill.

In Sherwell Church, which is opposite Plymouth Library, there is a lovely stained-glass window depicting the departure of the Pilgrims.

Many American troops were stationed in Plymouth during World War II, and from here they set out for the memorable D-Day landings. A plaque commemorating their departure for the Normandy Beach on June 6, 1944, was unveiled in 1958 by the then American Ambassador to Great Britain, Mr. John Hay Whitney. The plaque is set in a striking arrangement of stones.

Since the War, the old seaport of Plymouth has been largely rebuilt, and now has many modern buildings. Its Civic Center, Museum, Art Gallery, and shopping center are especially worth visiting.

In Exeter, a few miles northeast of Plymouth, is the famed Mol's Coffee House, where sea-dogs Drake, Hawkins, Gilbert, and Raleigh used to gather. A visit to this famous old Coffee House, now converted into an art shop, will be as interesting as a tour of the beautiful Exeter Cathedral, which it adjoins.

5

William Penn and the Quakers

There was a "Penn country" in Buckinghamshire, England, as early as 1273. On the west border of the county, where it adjoins Oxfordshire, was a little cluster of houses and a church named Penn. It is situated on a headland, or "pen" of the Chiltern Hills, hence the name. Penns lived here as long ago as the thirteenth century, for in 1273, Hugh de Penn presented the rectory of Penn to one William de London.

The William Penn that is famous in American history, however, was born on Tower Hill, in a court adjoining London Wall, in 1644. His father, Sir William Penn, was an admiral of the British Navy, under both royal and Cromwellian rule. At an early age, young Penn was sent to a preparatory school at Chigwell, which he attended until he was twelve. Then for four years he lived with his parents on the Penn estates in County Cork, Ireland, where he was privately tutored. It was here that he first heard Quaker preaching, by a tradesman named Thomas Loe.

At the age of sixteen, young Penn was accepted at Christ Church, Oxford, but he was more distinguished for his athletic abilities than for his scholarship. What was more significant, however, was that Thomas Loe, himself an Oxford man, turned up again. He and the other students argued about the established church and its form of worship, and some of them refused to attend services, holding meetings for worship of their own. They were fined, and it is not clear whether young William Penn was expelled officially or whether he decided to quit on his own volition. He later spoke of his "persecution" at Oxford and says he was "banished to college."

This sort of thing was embarrassing to his father's career, and there was considerable gossip in polite society. As Pepys said in his Diary, "There were too many bodies of excited revivalists with queer notions, and the Quakers were the worst of the lot, making a nuisance of themselves all over the country — refusing to take an oath and even to take off their hats, arguing with clergymen in their own churches, ridiculing the bishops, criticizing the general behavior of the public, and breaking the laws. Thousands of them were in prison and many had died there, but no kind of punishment seemed to be effective."

So young Penn was sent on a tour of the Continent. He stayed awhile in France and Italy before returning to England, where he studied law for awhile. He also attended his father on board ship, carried dispatches to King Charles II, and spent some time in military service in Ireland.

Persecuted for his faith, young Penn found staunch friends in the Pennington family and went frequently to their home at Chalfont St. Peter's, five or six miles from the village of Penn. Here the Quakers were always welcome. In the village church he could see memorials to his ancestors, beginning with the names of John Penn (died in 1597) and his wife Ursula.

The same year (1668) in which Penn met Isaac Pennington, he also appeared as a preacher and as the author of the essay, "The Sandy Foundation Shaken." Because of this essay he was imprisoned in the Tower of London for seven months, and during this time he wrote his most celebrated work *No Cross, No Crown,* as well as *Innocency with her Open Face.*

In 1670, Penn's father died, leaving him considerable property. There is a monument to Admiral Penn in the Church of St. Mary Redcliffe, in Bristol. During that same year the meetings of dissenters were forbidden by law, and severe penalties were prescribed for anyone breaking this law. The Quakers continued to meet, however, and again Penn found himself in prison. This time he spent six months at Newgate Prison because he refused to take the oath at his trial. During this period of confinement he wrote *The Great Case of Liberty of Conscience* and other pamphlets.

During his famous trial, Penn so eloquently defended the right of an English jury to render a verdict free of intimidation from the court that the jury acquitted him despite the guilty verdict directed by the court. The jury was then imprisoned, and this incident led to the famous Bushell case, in which the rights of English jurors were affirmed — a landmark in the development of English law.

In the spring of 1672, Penn married the very attractive Gulielma Maria Springett, stepdaughter of Isaac Pennington. Penn's religious fervor remained at a high pitch, and he continued to write and preach in England, Holland, and Germany. In 1672, Charles II issued the Declaration of Indulgence, whereby violent persecution of dissenters was brought to an end.

Although he continued to write and carry on his Quaker missionary work, Penn was now free to think of other things. He had long hoped to find in the New World a haven where complete freedom of conscience might be exercised.

The Crown owed Penn's late father about £16,000, and Penn persuaded the King to settle this debt by giving him land in the New World. As a result, on March 4, 1681, Charles II signed a charter by which "Pensilvania" was granted to William Penn as "true and absolute" proprietor and governor. This tract of land was almost as large as Britain itself. The land was given not only to settle the debt but also in gratitude for the elder Penn's assistance, as Admiral of the British Navy, in restoring Charles II to the throne.

Penn was not in favor of the title given to his possessions "lest it should be looked upon as vanity in me," but his scruples were over-ruled. He took pains to explain that the King had insisted on the name as a tribute to his father. Penn's own idea was that the colony should be called New Wales.

The graves of William Penn and his first wife, in the cemetery at Jordan's.

When this was rejected, however, he suggested Sylvania, and this the King accepted if it were prefixed by Penn. So Pennsylvania it was.

Although he did not abandon his religious crusading, Penn now became absorbed with such political questions as the "rights of men" and "freedom of conscience under the law." Although he had absolute rule in Pennsylvania and might well have excluded any settlers who did not follow his own beliefs, such a concept ran counter to his convictions. The first Frame of Government that he drafted for Pennsylvania in 1682 contained fundamental provisions designed to "put the power in the people."

Penn had confidence in the spirit of man as a reflection and interpretation of the spirit of God, if faithfully perceived, but he was perhaps too optimistic about the innate goodness of man being able to surmount all obstacles to achieve good government. "Governments, like clocks, go from the motion men give them," he stated in the preamble to his constitution for Pennsylvania,

The graves of Thomas and Mary Ellwood, in the cemetery at Jordan's

"and as governments are made and moved by men, so by them are they ruined too. Wherefore governments rather depend upon men than men upon governments. Let men be good, and the government cannot be bad. If it be ill, they will cure it. But if men be bad, let the government be ever so good, they will endeavor to warp and spoil it to their turn."

Unable to come to the province immediately, Penn sent his cousin, William Markham, with instructions to set the governmental machinery in motion. Penn arrived on October 29, 1682, and called a general assembly for December 4. At this meeting, Pennsylvania's first legal code, the Great Law, was enacted, in which primary emphasis was placed on freedom of conscience. A second assembly met in the new town of Philadelphia in March, 1683. When certain assembly leaders objected to some of the provisions of the first Frame of Government, Penn allowed them to draft a second, which was even more liberal than the first. He thus refrained from exercising the great

powers granted him under the charter. Like all Quakers, Penn believed in the dignity and worth of the individual, and relied upon the inner guiding light of conscience. Thus his writings on the problems of government have a distinctly religious flavor. He believed that if governments are to achieve success, they must depend upon the ability of men to be good. This belief in the common brotherhood and worth of all men had many practical consequences, notably in his remarkably just treaties with the Indians.

When Penn arrived in his new colony, the Indians greeted him in their canoes, and the traditional story is that he walked with them on the bank, ate their roasted acorns and hominy, and joined in their exuberant hopping and jumping games by leaping as high as any of them — a man of thirty-eight, still agile, and anxious to demonstrate his friendship in a way they could understand.

The presentation and explanation of the treaty evoke one of the most romantic scenes in the history of colonization. Penn arranged to meet at least three of the Indian tribes at a place on the river called Shackamaxon, which was a traditional assembly ground, the Place of Kings. Penn stepped ashore and strode to a clearing where the Indians awaited him, squatting in a wide semi-circle around an elm tree. The chiefs rose and an old warrior, Taminent, acted as spokesman. He announced, through an interpreter, that they were ready to hear the words of him whom they called Onas, the Iroquois word for quill or pen. All weapons were placed on the ground and the chiefs sat cross-legged to listen. Penn behaved toward them with the courtesy and deference that he would have shown to English royalty at Whitehall.

Penn addressed the gathering. "The Great Spirit who made me and you, who rules the heavens and the earth, and who knows the innermost thoughts of men, knows that I and my friends have a hearty desire to live in peace and friendship with you, and to serve you to the utmost of our power. It is not our custom to use hostile weapons against our fellow creatures, for which reason we have come unarmed. Our object is not to do injury, and thus provoke the Great Spirit, but to do good."

Following Taminent's instruction, one of the chiefs stepped forward to take Penn's hand and then replied to the effect that they agreed to the treaty, that there was friendship between them,

50

and that they wished to live together in amity "as long as the sun and moon shall endure."

The terms of the treaty were handed down among the Indians generation by generation, with reverence and understanding, and as long as the Quakers dominated the government in Pennsylvania, the treaty was not broken and the peaceful relationship between settlers and Indians astonished the other territories.

Penn stayed two years in the colony, until a boundary dispute with Maryland forced him to return to England in 1684. After the death of Charles II in 1685, Penn became a chief advisor to James II, who had long been his friend. When James was dethroned in 1688, Penn found himself in ill favor with William and Mary, James's successors. In 1692, he was suspended as governor of Pennsylvania, although retaining ownership of the land. His governing rights were restored in 1694, but he did not return to Pennsylvania until 1699.

During the intervening fifteen years there had been tremendous development in the colony, but there were also serious dissensions among the settlers. There was also the question of piracy, which Friends had been accused of encouraging because of their reluctance to use force, and the dilemma of reconciling conscience with the King's request to build fortifications for defence, in union with other colonies.

The major development of his second visit was another Frame of Government called the Charter of Privileges of 1701, which gave still greater powers of self-government to the province. This charter is considered one of the great documents in the history of freedom in America.

This visit also lasted two years, and every moment seems to have been spent in business, except for the pleasure of building himself a mansion four miles beyond Bristol on the Delaware, surrounded by gardens and lawns, with an avenue of poplars, as well as hawthorn and fruit trees sent out from England. Whether or not Penn would have made his home in Pennsylvania is questionable. His mind was made up for him by events in England which demanded his presence. Efforts were being made in Parliament to annex private colonies to the Crown, and friends urged him to return before the bill became a law.

Therefore in 1701 Penn was again forced to return to England. He had now become the greatest champion of religious freedom of his time,

and he had founded a colony devoted to recognizing religious toleration. His beliefs, which were contrary to those then prevailing, became central to those that later developed in the modern world. Unfortunately, his last years were marred by illness and debt, for which he was imprisoned for a time.

William Penn's last years were spent in the village of Ruscombe, near the Berkshire border, where he died in 1718. His death followed a six-year period of paralysis and amnesia, following a stroke in 1712. During this time his second wife, Hannah, looked after his affairs. The Indians of Pennsylvania, who had been constantly on his mind, sent their condolences to his widow and a gift of skins to make a cloak. With the death of Onas they had lost a protector and a friend in whose word they could trust.

William Penn and many of his family were buried at Jordans, a village in Buckinghamshire that is within easy driving distance from London. There, in the burial ground which was consecrated to the peace of death in 1671, one may see the graves of William Penn and his two wives and several of his children, as well as those of such well known Quakers as Thomas Ellwood and Isaac Pennington.

Jordans lies midway between the two Chalfonts, at the west end of the parish of Chalfont St. Giles, at the point where it is joined by the lane from Chalfont St. Peters. It is a lonely spot, but it has become one of the show places of the Quakers. The keynote of the place is silence and peace, both so befitting a fellowship whose worship is silence, whose watchword is peace, and whose principle of life is simplicity. Nothing simpler could mark the resting place of one who fought for peace and good will, who left a name and an influence on two continents, and whose life work is still marching on. There is no ambitious monument to mark William Penn's grave, merely a small stone with his name and the date of his death. His two wives, Gulielma and Hannah, lie by his side, while nearby are the graves of his children.

It is a striking instance of longevity: William Penn, born in 1644, in the reign of Charles I, and his grandson, Granville, the last Penn to own Stoke Park, who died in 1844, seven years after Queen Victoria ascended the throne. Thus the lives of father, son, and grandson covered exactly two hundred years.

The meetinghouse at Jordan's.

Jordans is only six or seven miles from Stoke Poges, made famous by Gray's "Elegy in a Country Churchyard." Inside the church is a tablet on which are inscribed the names of many of the Penn family, and the entrance to the Penn Vault is close to the font. The Stoke Poges Manor House was bought by Thomas Penn, son of William, in 1760 and was the home of the Penn family until 1840.

The parish church of Chalfont St. Giles also has Penn associations. This church contains architecture of four periods: parts of the chancel wall and window are Saxon; the pillars and part of the tower are Norman; the nave is early Gothic; and the Hastings Chapel, or the red-brick part, is Tudor. The Hastings Chapel, dating from 1550, is the part of the church that the visitor first approaches. It was originally built for the inmates of an almshouse, or hospital, which then stood quite near the church and which had been built by Lord Hastings in 1557. The original hospital was pulled down in 1765 by Thomas Penn, who replaced it by another Almshouse, which stands about a quarter of a mile to the north of the church.

In 1671, William Russell sold to the Quakers a quarter of an acre of land which adjoined his farm at Jordans. There, the Quakers built a meeting house in 1688. It is a plain brick structure, with a high-pitched roof, now partially covered with creepers. The interior is quaintly simple in its fittings and furniture, being panelled with plain, unvarnished oak and having high-backed benches of the same durable material, no doubt made in this fashion to remind the worshipper that this was no place for lolling or inattention. At one end is a raised platform with a few seats, while at the opposite end, a little below the ceiling, is a row of movable panels, behind which is a small "secret" chamber. In the days of informers and persecution, this was used by the women, and when the panels were closed, there was nothing to indicate the presence of listeners behind them. In case of disturbance by informers or others, the women could withdraw unobserved or remain concealed until the trouble was over. On the merest hint that intruders were about, the sliding panels could be closed, and a mouse-like stillness observed.

John Pennington, Thomas Ellwood, and five

Interior of the meetinghouse at Jordan's.

other Friends saw to the building of the meeting house at their joint expense. Local craftsmen built it of local materials. Its brickwork is of the Flemish type common in Buckinghamshire, with black header bricks lying end-on between the red stretcher bricks. Its plain, hipped roof still has many of the local tiles.

The building consists of the main meeting house, which takes about two-thirds of the floor area and the full height, and a two-storeyed cottage for a caretaker at the eastern end, with some stables behind. From the beginning, the cottage served a dual purpose in order to allow extra room for crowded meetings. The lower part of the cottage has an anteroom, in which the original fireplace is preserved. The upper part became a gallery overlooking the meeting room and today housing an interesting collection of documents and pictures. Modifications and extensions were made several times, in 1867, 1941, and 1958.

The interior of the meeting house, however, is essentially the same as when it was first built. Much of the window furniture and glass are original. The panelling and the raised minister's

The minister's gallery, in the meetinghouse at Jordan's.

The home at Jordan's where Penn often visited.

stand probably date from 1733. The floor is of unmortared, close-fitting paving bricks laid on the bare earth. Originally, the plain unvarnished benches were arranged in rows facing the minister's stand, but in 1963 they were turned to face inwards.

The turbulent years of Oliver Cromwell, 1646-1660, saw the rise of the Quaker movement. Following the restoration of the monarchy under Charles II, there emerged, out of bitterness and dissension, the Conventicle Act of 1664, which forbade religious meetings of more than five persons, and the Five Mile Act of 1665, which prohibited the residence of non-conformist ministers and teachers within five miles of a town, unless they had taken oaths against any alteration of church and state. Persecution, especially of Quakers, was rife, although it varied in harshness from one district to another. Informers flourished. Many Quakers were imprisoned.

The Declaration of Indulgence, which James II was forced to make, stopped the direct persecution of Friends and other non-conformists. The Toleration Act of William and Mary ended fines and imprisonment for attending Meeting. Friends took advantage at once of the changed conditions and took out licenses for more than a hundred permanent meeting-houses. This one at Jordans was one of the hundred.

Old Jordans is on the hill above the meeting house. Although it shows the wear and tear of years and usage, the original farmhouse of the Russell family is still intact and includes the room, built in 1624, where the early Friends worshipped. The Quakers bought it from St. Luke's Hospital, London, in 1911. In 1912, the old farmhouse was converted into a Hostel, to be used as a center for rest and inspiration, and has been so used ever since.

Along the west side is the Refectory, with eight bedrooms on the upper floor. Originally there were stables on this site, but they were converted into a large reception room with attic above, during World War I. This original refectory was burned down in 1962 and the replacement built in 1970.

The peaceful charm of the garden and the beauty of the surrounding Chiltern Hills are all conducive to refreshment of mind and spirit. The rooms of the Hostel are well furnished, all with central heating or electric fires, and hot and cold running water. The meals are of a high standard, but no alcoholic drinks are served. The new refectory and the Mayflower Barn are available for meetings, lectures, and such social occasions as wedding receptions. Trains run frequently from Marlyebone Station, in London, to Seer Green Station, which is three-quarters of a mile from the Hostel. It is an easy drive of twenty-one miles from Jordans to London, on the Green Line route. Room and full board are available at moderate rates, and even non-residents may come here for meals. The use of the Hostel is not limited to Quakers.

Across the sunken garden is the Mayflower Barn, which dates from 1624. The Russell family, prosperous farmers, bought the timber of the *Mayflower* for fifty pounds and built the barn and a large kitchen. It is a large, typical Buckinghamshire barn, one of the best preserved of the few such barns remaining. Many of the roof tiles are no doubt original. As proof that it was originally the *Mayflower* one of the central beams has a repaired crack in it, and it is known that a beam of the *Mayflower* gave way during the adventurous voyage of the Pilgrim Fathers. Roughly cut into another beam are the letters R Har I, which may be part of MayfloweR HARwIch. The English, as well as Americans, like to think of the Mayflower Barn as a sentimental tie with America and an item of old, rustic, functional beauty that has endured in loving hands through more than three centuries.

William Penn was a frequent visitor to Old

The Guest House at Jordan's.

Jordans, as were Thomas Ellwood and George Fox, leading Quakers of their day. About eight to ten thousand visitors come to Jordans each year, from all over the world. The summer concerts held in the Mayflower Barn during July and August attract a crowd of over three hundred for each concert.

The Mayflower Barn, at Jordan's.

The interior of the Mayflower Barn.

In 1881, the then Governor of Pennsylvania planned a national memorial to William Penn. He asked permission to remove Penn's remains to Philadelphia, pointing out that they lay in a disused burial ground near an infrequently used meeting-house and that Pennsylvania, indeed all America, owed much to William Penn. The Society of Friends declined the request and there were several more requests, and much correspondence in *The Times* of London. American Quakers were inclined to support the proposal, but English Quakers believed it was contrary to the spirit in which Penn had lived and to his request to be buried at Jordans. The English stood firm and Penn's remains were not disturbed.

6

Elihu Yale and John Harvard

Elihu Yale, for whom Yale University is named, was born in or near Boston, Mass., on April 5, 1648. He was the second son of David Yale, who came from an old English family and had emigrated with his stepfather, Theophilus Eaton, to New Haven, Conn., on the founding of that colony, but had afterwards settled in Boston.

David Yale returned to England in 1652 and settled in London, when Elihu was only four years old. Nothing is known of Elihu's education, but when he was about twenty-two years old he went out to India in the service of the East India Company and remained there until 1699. In 1687, he became governor of the company settlement at Fort St. George, Madras. In 1692, however, he lost his position as governor because of having engaged in private trade, which was not deemed proper for one in his position. Had it not been for this, however, he would probably not have retired with the sizable fortune that he amassed.

Upon his return to England in 1699, Yale became a governor of the East India Company, a company made famous by the men who fought with a free right hand for themselves (thus establishing the foundations of great fortunes) and with the left hand added the islands and continents that became known as the British Empire.

The Yale family came originally from Wales and had lived for generations in the old manor house of Plas yn Yale, about two miles northeast of Bryn Eglwys. That they were a dominant family and occupied a position comparable to that of an English squire is demonstrated by the fact that in the little church of Bryn Eglwys is a small transept

known as the Yale Chapel. Several generations of Yales worshipped in this church.

There was undoubtedly something of a fine old style about this Welsh gentleman with the high-handed ways, who quarrelled with the Council at Madras and with the governors at home, but who combined the activities of merchant, adventurer, and official, made a notable fortune, and then scattered it with a wise and abundant liberality. The library of St. Paul's School contains a number of volumes that were a gift from Elihu Yale, and the fine old parish church of Wrexham, the largest town in the county of his ancestors, was the recipient of many gifts from him, including the Altar Piece representing the institution of the Sacrament.

It may have been Yale's reputation for generosity that caused Cotton Mather to invite him to help the struggling Collegiate School of Connecticut, which was first established at Saybrook and later moved to New Haven. Yale sent over a large quantity of books, pictures, and other effects, the sale of which brought a considerable sum. In gratitude, the trustees of the college changed its name to Yale. Later, by the charter of 1745, the entire institution was named Yale University, in honor of Elihu Yale, its greatest benefactor.

Yale died in London on July 8, 1721, and was buried on July 22 in the churchyard of the Church of St. Giles, in Wrexham, in northeastern Wales, about twenty-five miles south of Liverpool. His epitaph reads:

The tomb of Elihu Yale, in the churchyard of the Church of St. Giles, in Wrexham, Wales.

Born in America, in Europe bred,
In Africa travelled, and in Asia wed;
Where long he lived and thrived,
  In London died.
Much good, some ill, he did, so hope all's even
And that his soul through mercy's gone to
heaven.
  You that survive and read this tale, take care
For this most certain exit to prepare,
When, blest in peace, the actions of the just
  Smell sweet and blossom in the dust!

In 1870 and again in 1895, the tomb was restored and newly inscribed by the Corporation of Yale College, "in grateful remembrance of his timely aid in money and other values." Besides this monument to Elihu Yale in the churchyard, the chancel of St. Giles contains tablets to members of the Yale family, which was of considerable importance in this part of Wales. These memorials include brasses to Elihu's father and to his brother David.

Yale married Catherine Hymners and they had one son and three daughters. The son died in Madras, but the three daughters all married. The youngest, Catherine, married Dudley North, whose great-grandson, the last descendant of Elihu Yale, presented Yale University with the portrait of his great-grandfather in 1789. The portrait was painted in 1717 by a Dutch artist, Enoch Zeeman, a resident of England.

John Harvard was born in 1607 not far from the Globe Theatre, in Southwark, a borough of London, and baptized at St. Saviour's Church on November 20 of that year. His father, Robert Harvard, was a butcher who lived and carried on his business in the High Street, Southwark, near the ancient collegiate church of St. Saviour (St. Mary Overy), now known as Southwark Cathedral.

The Harvard home was directly east of the Lady Chapel, and the old "Token Books" indicate its number and location in ancient maps. These tokens were small circular pieces of lead which were distributed by the church wardens to parishioners over the age of fifteen or sixteen as a summons to attend Holy Communion. When the rite had been duly honored, the tokens were given back to the officers of the church. Thus, no one could shirk his religious duty without being found out. It was a strange system and may have been one factor in the revulsion that later caused so many people like the Harvards to cross the water to a land of freer views and larger ways.

Robert, the butcher, had gone to Stratford-on-Avon in 1605, and that year had married Katharine Rogers, his second wife, whose father was an alderman of Stratford. The ornate, half-timbered house which Thomas Rogers built in 1596, and where John Harvard's mother grew up, may still be seen, on High Street, in Stratford-on-Avon. Harvard House is now the property of Harvard University, and is open to visitors.

As a result of the plague in 1625, which made sad ravages in the family, John Harvard's mother left the old house in Southwark and lived in Tower Hill with a new husband. From here, John went to Emmanuel College, Cambridge, in 1627. When she lost her second husband, Mrs. Harvard returned to Southwark and married Richard Yearwood, a friend of her first husband. She spent the rest of her days in a house that was within a few doors of the old home in High Street, Southwark.

John Harvard remained at Cambridge for eight years, taking his B.A. degree in 1631 and his M.A. in 1635. Shortly thereafter he married Ann, the daughter of the Rev. John Sadler, a Sussex clergyman, and in 1637 they migrated to New England. This was only seventeen years after the Pilgrims had set up their first tabernacle in the wilderness. Now thirty years old, John Harvard was appointed minister to the first church in Charlestown.

A year before he arrived, the colonists had started a project for the establishment of a college for the education of English and Indian youth in "knowledge and godliness." When Harvard heard of this scheme it aroused his interest and sympathy, and he bequeathed it half his fortune, amounting to nearly eight hundred pounds. He also gave his library of three hundred and twenty volumes. Such a gift practically set the project on its feet. Newtown had been chosen as the site of the institution, but in recognition of John

A plaque in Southwark, London, indicating the site of the Harvard home.

Harvard's beneficence, it was changed to Cambridge, as a tribute of respect to the university that he had attended in England. It was also decided to call their humble seminary after the name of its chief founder and benefactor. John Harvard died of tuberculosis a year after his arrival in New England. The place of his burial is unknown.

For nearly two centuries, nothing was known of Harvard's ancestry or place of birth. Finally, Henry F. Waters discovered his connection with Southwark and the cathedral church of the diocese, now known as Southwark Cathedral. "As I passed through this venerable edifice," he wrote, "I noticed that the great window in the south transept was of plain glass, as if Providence had designed that some day the sons of Harvard should place there a worthy memorial to one who is so well entitled to their veneration."

Harvard House, in Stratford-on-Avon, where John Harvard's mother grew up.

Southwark Cathedral, London.

The challenge was not taken up, however, until the Hon. Joseph H. Choate, then Ambassador to England and himself a Harvard graduate, was seized with the desire to add one more to the array of monuments and memorials to great and noteworthy men. The offer of a memorial window to John Harvard was gratefully accepted by the rector and in due course a beautiful stained-glass window, the work of J. LaFarge of New York, was placed in the chapel of St. John the Divine, later known as the Harvard Memorial Chapel.

The main subject of the window is the baptism of Christ (an allusion to the baptism of John Harvard in this church). This scene occupies the lower central panel and has two angels in attendance, one on either hand. A panel of old stained glass occupies the middle center and is flanked on each side by the arms of Harvard University and Emmanuel College, Cambridge. The whole makes a striking contrast to the other stained-glass windows in the church, partly from the fact that the leading follows the folds of the drapery and the shaded lines of the figures, thus avoiding the breaking up of the picture into a number of rectangular spaces. This memorial was formally unveiled by Mr. Choate just before his departure from England in May, 1905, in the presence of the Archbishop of Canterbury, the Bishop of Rochester, Canon Thompson (the rector); Dr. Butler, Master of Trinity College, Cambridge, and many others.

After drawing aside the American flag which covered the window, Mr. Choate said that it was nearly three centuries since John Harvard was baptized in that church. Educated at Emmanuel College, Cambridge, during the same years that Milton was attending Christ's College, the two must have received substantially the same nurture and discipline, and were no doubt occasionally thrown together. At any rate, said Mr. Choate, John Harvard and John Milton must have imbibed something of the same spirit, for Milton's contemporaries spoke of him as a scholar and pious in his life.

Speaking of the coat-of-arms adopted by the college, possibly at the suggestion of John Harvard, Mr. Choate said: "It assumed on its coat-of-arms a double motto, *Veritas,* truth — a word broad enough to embrace all knowledge, human and divine — and *Christo et Ecclesiae,* for Christ and Church. Now, after a lapse of three centuries, the little college in the pathless wilderness has become a great and splendid university, strong in prestige and renown, rich in endowments, and richer still in the pious loyalty of its sons. It is not unworthy to be compared with Oxford and Cambridge, those ancient nurseries of learning from which it drew for its first life. And the name of John Harvard shares the fame which mankind accords to the founders of states. . .Thus, the name of John Harvard, unknown and of little account when he left England, has been a benediction to the New World, and his timely and generous act has born fruit a millionfold."

Within two years of the unveiling of the memorial window, the restoration of the ancient chapel of St. John the Divine was completed by the sons of Harvard College. Since then it has been called the Harvard Memorial Chapel. Mr. Choate also expressed the hope that this chapel would long remain for Americans a place of pilgrimage to remind them "where one of their proudest institutions had its origin."

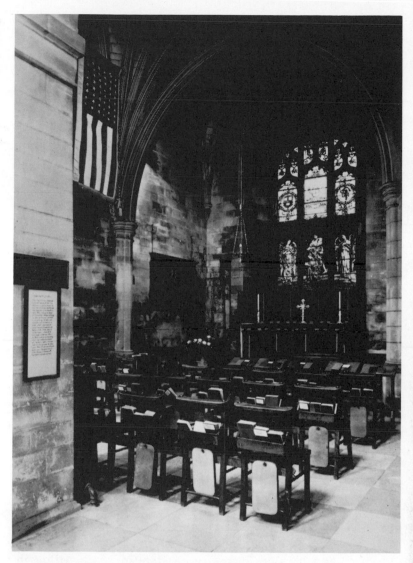

Harvard Chapel in Southwark Cathedral, London.

7

Calvert and Oglethorpe: Founders of States

Yorkshire not only supplied the humble folk who became the Pilgrims, but it was also the birthplace of the Calverts, father and son, who were responsible for the colonizing of Maryland. George Calvert, the father, was born in 1580 in the village of Kipling, near Northallerton, Yorkshire. Northallerton, which lies 32 miles northwest of York, is thought to have been occupied in Roman times. The town is dominated by the parish Church of All Saints, and nearby is the old Porch House, where Charles I was imprisoned for a time.

In 1604, George Calvert married Anne Mynne, who was born at Hertingfordbury, near Hertford, Hertfordshire. Calvert entered Parliament in 1609 and became Secretary of State in 1619. Although he resigned from Parliament in 1625, Calvert did not lose the confidence of the King, James I, who conferred on him the title of Baron and gave him large estates in County Longford, Ireland. From this time on, Lord Baltimore (Calvert's new title) gave up affairs of state and concentrated on colonization.

In 1623, Calvert had obtained a charter to found a colony in Newfoundland under the name of the province of Avalon, in imitation of old Avalon in Somersetshire, where Glastonbury stands, the reputed scene of the beginnings of Christianity in Britain.

Calvert crossed the ocean in 1627 and again in 1629, taking his family with him to Newfoundland. He found the climate too trying and the hostility of the French too unpleasant so he gave up the idea of a colony in Newfoundland.

As one of the original members of the Virginia Company, Calvert visited the colony in 1631. At that time, he observed that there was no settlement north of the Potomac River, and he thought there should be one. He made up his mind to obtain a grant of land and to colonize it with people of his own faith (Roman Catholic), who were being severely persecuted in England at that time.

The King tried to talk him out of the idea, but finally gave in and, in 1632, gave Calvert a grant of land that later became the state of Maryland. Before the charter was formally issued, however, George Calvert died. The land was inherited by his son Cecil, who thus became the founder of the colony.

Cecil Calvert, now Lord Baltimore, immediately appointed his brother Leonard governor. Leonard Calvert, with two hundred English settlers, sailed for Maryland in November, 1632, and landed the following February near the mouth of the Potomac.

The colony was well managed and made more progress in six months than Virginia had done in six years, largely owing to the kindly way in which Calvert treated the Indians. Cecil Calvert himself never visited the colony, though he remained its proprietor for forty-three years, until his death in 1675. During that time the Toleration Act was passed, which gave the colony a religious freedom that was rare in those days.

The colony was named Maryland after Queen Henriette Maria, wife of Charles I. Arundel County was named for Calvert's wife, Anne Arundel. Baltimore, of course, was named for the first Lord Baltimore, George Calvert. The name Baltimore came originally from an estate in County Longford, Ireland. In a few generations there were no more Baltimores, and the family became extinct.

When Cromwell ruled England, the government of Maryland had its troubles, which were not overcome until Charles was restored to the throne. At this time, Lord Baltimore appointed his son Charles as governor. He succeeded in establishing peace and prosperity in the colony, but only for a season. The fact that he was a Catholic continued to cause him trouble.

Lord Baltimore was buried in St. Dunstan's-in-the-West, on Fleet Street, London (EC 3). This octagon-shaped church was founded in the 13th century but rebuilt in 1829-33 and repaired in 1950. The tower was an open-work lantern inspired by that of All Saints' Pavement at York. Over the vestry porch there is a statue of Elizabeth I dating from 1586. The northwest window of the church shows Izaak Walton, who was a vestryman of the church in 1629-44, and the subjects of his *Lives*. *The Compleat Angler* was first published in St. Dunstan's churchyard in 1653. John Donne, the poet, was vicar here from 1624 until his death in 1631.

James Edward Oglethorpe, the founder of Georgia, was born in London and baptized at St. Martins-in-the-Fields, on Trafalgar Square, on December 23, 1696. He joined the army in 1710 and entered Parliament in 1722 as a member from Haslemere, Surrey. Oglethorpe was interested in penal reform and in 1729 became chairman of the Parliamentary committee investigating debtors' prisons. The result was the establishment of the royal colony of Georgia as a refuge for paupers, with Oglethorpe appointed as governor.

On October 30, 1732, he sailed on the *Anne* to the Virginia Colony and the following year he founded the town of Savannah, Georgia. Oglethorpe won the friendship of the Indians and was able for a long time to defend the new colony against the Spaniards, but met his great defeat at St. Augustine, Florida, in 1740.

The British government had given General Oglethorpe a grant of land extending from the Savannah River to the Altamaha. From the day that the General set foot in Spanish territory, it was inevitable that the British and the Spanish interests would clash head on. The Spanish claimed that the British monarch had no right to bestow on any of his subjects the lands south of Port Royal Sound (in southern South Carolina). In defiance of this treaty, Oglethorpe set up a chain of forts south to the St. John's River (in northern Florida).

With South Carolina terrorized by the slave insurrection at Stono in September, 1739, Oglethorpe scarcely needed a provocation when the Spaniards from St. Augustine landed on Amelia Island and killed two sick Highlanders.

Oglethorpe's attack on St. Augustine in 1740 was preceded by elaborate preparations. On New Year's Day, 1740, he destroyed Fort Piccolata and captured Fort San Francisco de Pupa, which was a wooden fort built like a blockhouse. Then he blockaded the St. John's River, thus cutting off possible aid (to St. Augustine) from friendly Indians to the west and north, as well as preventing the regular movements of the Spanish patrols on that river and along the coast northward to the St. Mary's River.

Having taken these steps, he sent requests to the English colonies in the West Indies for reinforcements. He also secured a promise from Admiral Vernon of the English fleet in the Caribbean to keep the Spaniards in Havana and the West Indies fully occupied with problems of their own, so that they would not send aid to St. Augustine.

With a contingent of 220 of his own men and 125 Carolinians, Oglethorpe landed at Fort St. George, just south of the St. John's River, on May 9, 1740. With a part of his force, he pushed down to within twenty-five miles of St. Augustine and captured Fort Diego and fifty men on May 12. Then he dashed down to the Inlet of St. Augustine, within sight of the city, fired some guns, and marched back to Fort Diego on May 16. On May 18, he returned to the St. John's River. To men drinking bad water and marching in the sand over palmetto roots under terrific heat, these fruitless marches were just too much.

Meanwhile, the sea captains notified Oglethorpe that they could not remain longer than July 5, for fear of hurricanes which came at this time of year. On June 12, Oglethorpe crossed over to Anastasia Island, leaving the Carolina regiment on the other side of the Inlet. The Carolina officers were disappointed at this division of forces, for to them it showed a lack of aggressive intentions. They had expected to follow the example of Colonel Moore, who in 1702 had driven the 2,400 inhabitants of

Air view of the old fort in St. Augustine, Florida.

St. Augustine into the fort and captured it by dropping bombs.

The Spaniards had not been idle, however. They had the advantage of being familiar with the harbor and the tides. As a result, they had anchored many small vessels safely out of the range of the English guns, yet in such a position as to prevent the English from carrying out their plans to enter the harbor and plant shore batteries.

As a result of these Spanish defenses, Oglethorpe was forced to convert his planned assault into a siege. The Carolina colonies sent him a body of four hundred troops and he also equipped a body of Creek Indians. In May, he rendezvoused at the mouth of the St. John's River a force of two thousand men. They also had six vessels of war, equipped with heavy cannon and landing parties for siege operations.

The Spaniards, however, duly warned by Oglethorpe's activities in the St. John's River Valley, had guessed his intentions and secured naval as well as military reinforcements. At dawn on June 15, the Spaniards surprised Oglethorpe's contingent and swept over it with such impetuosity that they routed the English, killing fifty or sixty men, taking twenty-odd prisoners, and scattering the rest, wounded and half-naked, into the woods.

Since Oglethorpe never made the sudden attack he had promised in Charleston, nor the prolonged siege he suggested as a substitute for quick success, he probably never had any plan after landing at St. George's. His critics at the time said that he should have landed his forces behind the city and choked the city and fort off from the inland. Instead, he had marched his men, without proper supplies, along the coast in sight of the Spanish warships.

Without consulting anyone, Oglethorpe gave orders to abandon the siege and he went off in such haste as to abandon many provisions and war materials. One reason for Oglethrope's failure was

The altar and carved wood reredos in the chancel of St. Margaret's Church, London. Above the altar is the window honoring Sir Walter Raleigh.

Winston Churchill's home, Chartwell, near Westerham, Kent.

The Washington coat-of-arms in the window of the Great Hall of Sulgrave Manor.

Statue of Franklin D. Roosevelt in Grosvenor Square, London.

The American Memorial Chapel in St. Paul's Cathedral, London.

his refusal to call councils of war. He could have learned a great deal from the men who were experienced with the terrain and the American type of warfare—which Oglethorpe was not.

The siege of St. Augustine was finally abandoned on July 10. During the bombardment, 153 shells fell in the town but there was no loss of life.

Oglethorpe made a second attempt, in 1743, to capture the Spanish capital of Florida. This time he tried to coax the Spaniards out of the fort to attack him. Again he was unsuccessful, and he returned to England and never visited Georgia again.

Oglethorpe was highly criticized in London, and an official report was published about his failure. During the attack upon St. Augustine, Oglethorpe fell ill of a fever, and perhaps his irresolution and lack of definite plans for attack were the result of the illness that had already taken hold. James Oglethorpe died in 1785.

8

General Wolfe, Hero of Quebec

James Wolfe, the British general who won Quebec from the French, has long been a hero to all British Canadians. He was born on January 2, 1727, at the vicarage in Westerham, Kent, where his mother was staying for her confinement, while her husband was away with his regiment. The Wolfes had moved to what is now called Quebec House the year before and lived there until 1739, but in those days the house was known as Spiers, probably from its twelve steep gables, or spires. This imposing 17th century brick house, where Wolfe lived as a child, is not far from the center of Westerham. It is open to the public on certain days and contains an interesting collection of Wolfe, Montcalm, and other Quebec relics. Among the six thousand visitors each year, about one-third are Canadians.

Kent is a beautiful picturesque county immediately south of Greater London, and Westerham itself is a delectable little town in a district much favored by hikers. On Wolfe's birthday, January 2, a Wolfe Dinner is held in Westerham each year in honor of the town's hero. In 1911, a monument to Wolfe was erected on the village green showing him, with drawn sword, leading his men to victory.

Not far from Quebec House is the parish church of St. Mary the Virgin, where James Wolfe worshipped as a boy. The original Saxon church existed on this site as early as 1115, and there may be a trace or two of this early church in some lower courses of stone near the tower. There is no record of any Norman church having been here. The early English church was a simple structure comprising chancel, nave, and west tower with spire. The portions of this building still remaining are the chancel east wall, the great part of the tower and spire, and parts of the nave and chancel walls above the arcades. Toward the end of the 15th century, the church underwent a general reconstruction, and it was extended by adding the north and south aisles to the nave.

The ancient font, an example of early Decorated work, has an octagonal bowl supported on a niched shaft. In each face of the bowl is a quatre-foil-shaped recess with a plain shield. It was in this font that James Wolfe was baptized on January 11, 1727, when he was nine days old.

Several of the church windows are filled with attractive examples of modern stained glass, notably the chancel east window, designed by Henry Holiday. The Wolfe memorial window in the north wall is a pre-Raphaelite Annunciation scene executed in the William Morris workships after a design by Burne-Jones. The Wolfe memorial tablet over the south doorway bears an inscription in verse, probably written by the vicar, the Rev. George Lewis.

In 1739, Wolfe's family left Westerham and moved to a house at the top of Crooms Hill, in Greenwich. James attended school at Weston's Academy in King Street (now King William's Walk) in Greenwich. When he was fourteen, young Wolfe entered the British Army and soon rose to the rank of Second Lieutenant. Between 1742 and 1753, he served in Flanders, Germany, and Scotland. He was quarter-master general in Ireland, 1757-58, and at Rochefort, 1758.

During intervals of his military service, Wolfe stayed in his parents' home. On one of these visits, he met his next-door neighbor, Elizabeth Lawson, whom he loved and courted unsuccessfully for four unhappy years. Miss Lawson died, unmarried, in 1759. Wolfe's father died in that same year, only a few months before his son's triumph at Quebec.

During the French and Indian War in America, Wolfe commanded a brigade at Louisburg, in 1758, where he gave brilliant support to Jeffrey Amherst in the siege and capture of the fort. As a result, he was made major-general and commander of the British expedition sent to Canada to sieze power from the French, in 1759. After months of futile attempts to dislodge the forces of Montcalm from the well fortified city of Quebec, Wolfe conceived a brilliant strategy for taking the city. He landed his army at night on the Plains of Abraham, above the city, on September 12-13, and engaged the French in the battle which gave the English supremacy in Canada. Wolfe and Montcalm both lost their lives in this decisive battle.

General Wolfe's body was brought back from Quebec and laid to rest in the vault of St. Alphege's Church, in the center of Greenwich. The present St. Alphege's was the first church to be built as a result of the Fifty New Churches Act passed in 1712, in the reign of Queen Anne. There had been a church on the site since the 12th century, to mark the martyrdom of St. Alphege. In 1012, the Danes sacked Canterbury and captured the Archbishop Alphege at Greenwich. Alphege stoically refused to allow his people to pay the ransom demanded by the Danes, and this refusal led to his violent slaughter and subsequent canonization.

In time the parish church of Greenwich not only looked after the people of the village of Greenwich but also served the court and the palace of Tudor times, which were then located in Greenwich. Henry VIII was baptized in this church, while Edward VI, Queen Mary, and Queen Elizabeth I all attended services here, where Thomas Tallis was the Royal organist. Both Pepys and Evelyn were regular worshippers at St. Alphege's. Pepys commented, characteristically, "By coach to Greenwich Church, where a good sermon, a fine

Quebec House, in Westerham, Kent, the boyhood home of James Wolfe.

church, and a great company of handsome women."

In 1710, a violent storm caused the church to collapse, though the steeple remained standing. It was actually the petition of the Greenwich parishioners for a new church that caused Parliament to enact the Fifty New Churches Act of 1712, which was designed to meet the needs of a growing population in London and the suburbs. Greenwich was the first area to benefit, and only half the fifty churches were ever built.

Hawksmoor's Baroque design of St. Alphege's Church contrasts greatly with Wren's city churches, but of course Wren had been cramped by the limited space in which he was allowed to build a church in London. As a result, his churches concentrate their poise and beauty in their soaring steeples. Hawksmoor, on the other hand, took advantage of the open ground on either side and his church was placed in an Enclosure. . ."to keep off nastyness and Brutes," as he quaintly put it. The simplicity of his design gave it strength. The

The Church of St. Mary the Virgin, where Wolfe was baptized.

The statue of James Wolfe in Westerham.

St. Alphege's Church, in Greenwich, where Wolfe is buried.

The General Wolfe corner in St. Alphege's Church, Greenwich.

The plaque to General Wolfe in St. Alphege Church, Greenwich.

The statue of General Wolfe on a hilltop in Greenwich

main axis runs from east to west, with only gentle protusions on either side to form the transepts. The general effect is one of extraordinary harmony.

Unfortunately, an incendiary bomb in World War II destroyed most of the interior, which had carried out the architect's conception of fusing architecture, wood sculpture, and painting into an eloquent expression of faith. That is now lost and the interior seems colorless by comparison with its original state.

Despite the ravages of war, St. Alphege's is still an historic church of great beauty, where many notable persons have worshipped, from Lord Chesterfield to Queen Caroline.

At the top of a hill in Greenwich Park, near the Old Observatory, there is an imposing statue of General Wolfe by Tait Mackenzie. It overlooks the River Thames and a magnificent vista of London in the distance. The statue was presented by the Canadian nation before World War II to honor one of their greatest heroes. It was unveiled by the Marquis of Montcalm, a direct descendant of Wolfe's famous adversary at Quebec.

9

The Washingtons

The known story of the Washingtons in England goes back to the year 1183, when a William de Hertburn exchanged his village of Hertburn for the manor and village of Wessyngton, in the same diocese. The family changed its name along with its estate, and henceforth was known as the de Wessyngtons, the early Anglo-Saxon spelling of the name Washington. An American genealogist, Albert Welles, has traced the family back even further and says they derived from no less a hero than Odin, King of Scandinavia. In any case, they seem to have been of that good sound yeoman stock that played so large a part in the making of England and her colonies beyond the seas.

The Washington family roots are deep in the history of County Durham, in northeastern England. From 1183 until 1399, the senior branch of the family lived in Washington Old Hall, a small manor house set in the historic region of Northumbria between the cities of Newcastle-upon-Tyne and Durham. Actually, the Old Hall continued in the possession of Washington descendants until 1613, when it was sold to William James, Bishop of Durham. By this time, however, it had been the home of five generations of George Washington's direct ancestors.

Although Washington Old Hall dates from the twelfth century, it was largely rebuilt in the seventeenth century. Situated in Washington village on a small, pleasantly wooded hill next to the parish church, the house is a monument to Anglo-American friendship. In 1936, it fell on bad times and was threatened with demolition. A Preservation Committee was set up and generous gifts from both sides of the Atlantic saved the house and allowed restoration work to begin. During the restoration, it was found that not all the pre-17th century structure had been destroyed.

At the entrance to the grounds is a pair of 18th-century gates, presented by Chapter XI of the Colonial Dames of America. To the right of the gates is the caretaker's lodge, whose reconstruction was the gift of Mr. Charles Sumner Bird of Walpole, Massachusetts.

The building is H-shaped, with the Great Hall in the middle. In mediaeval times this would have been the communal dining room. The fireplace in the Great Hall, as well as the Yorkshire chairs and the heavy oak dining table, date from the early 17th century. At one end of the room stands the American flag, whose design is thought to have been inspired by the de Wessyngton coat-of-arms, which contained three stars and two stripes. Throughout the house, there are many items on display that are connected with George Washington, and many others associated with the district.

Through arches at the west end of the Great Hall one enters the kitchen. These arches have survived from the original 12th-century house. In the huge open fireplace of the kitchen there is a complex system of roasting jack and spits. The jack was turned by a vane placed in the throat of the chimney and rotated by the currents of hot air from the fire. On one side of the fireplace is a wedge-shaped opening revealing one of the original windows.

The Great Hall, in the center of the ancestral home, Washington Old Hall, in Northumbria, northern England.

At the east end of the Great Hall is a small withdrawing room, with Jacobean panelling from the old manor house at Abbots Langley. This panelling and some of the furniture were gifts of Miss Mabel Choate in memory of her father, who was American Ambassador to Great Britain. The cradle, the 17th-century wool-winder, and the lace or bible box help to give that "lived-in look" to the room.

After the original staircase was burned out some time ago, it was replaced with an intricately carved oak stairs, the gift of Lord and Lady Gort. The stairs lead to three rooms used by the people of Washington village as a community center. Throughout the house are pictures and other mementos of George Washington, including an eighteenth-century uniform of his personal body-guard, the Washington Greys; a bust of Washington by the French sculptor Houdon, who stayed with Washington at Mt. Vernon in 1785; a portrait of the President painted on parchment in 1776 by Joshua Trumbull of Salem, Massachusetts; a fan

presented to Martha Washington by Lafayette; and various other objects of interest.

On July 4 of each year, a ceremony is held here, marking the association with George Washington, while Old Glory is flown here on his birthday and Thanksgiving Day. Washington Old Hall is open throughout the year, except on Fridays. In 1975, Washington Old Hall was given by the National Trust of Great Britain to the American people as the first of several Bicentennial contributions by the mother country.

Washington was originally an agricultural village, and later the center of coal mining. Now it lies in the midst of a cleverly designed new town, while much of the surrounding land has been engulfed in the mining area of Durham County. The country-side, however, is still beautiful and there is much to see nearby. Only two miles to the east is Hylton Castle, built in the early fifteenth century. In this castle there is the oldest example of the Washington crest in stone. The open-air museum at Beamish, nine miles to the southwest, and the cathedral city of Durham, twelve miles away, are well worth a visit. In the cloisters of Durham Cathedral, there is a memorial plaque to John Washington, stating, "Prior of this Cathedral Church 1416-1446, whose family has won ever-lasting fame in lands to him unknown."

To link the Durham Washingtons with the first President of the United States, one must go back to Walter de Wessyngton, who fought with Henry III at the Battle of Lewes in 1264. Walter had three sons and from John, the youngest, George Washington is descended. John moved to a western county, married, and entered the feudal lordship of the family of Lancaster. His wife, Elizabeth, was the heiress of Gilbert de Burnside and the ruins of her home, Burnside Hall, are still standing, a mile north of Kendal in the Lakeland county of Westmoreland. John's eldest son, Robert, also married well, into the Strickland family, who lived then, as now, at Sizergh Castle, just south of Kendal.

The Lawrence Washington who was twice mayor of Northampton was obviously a man of some consequence. His mother was Margaret, daughter of Robert Kitson, of Warton. The Washington coat-of-arms may still be seen on the church tower of Warton. Margaret Washington was a sister of Sir Thomas Kitson, one of the most successful merchants of his time. This relationship to the

Kitsons had a most powerful influence upon the fortunes of the Washington family.

Lawrence Washington was trained to the law and studied at Gray's Inn in London. While still a young man, Lawrence turned his attention to commerce, probably on the advice of, and with the aid of, his uncle, Sir Thomas Kitson. He settled in Northampton where he became very prosperous and was twice elected mayor of that city.

Wool was the chief product of Northampton and of Warwick. Northampton was the center of the wool trade for that part of the country and its wool-combers were a thriving and energetic body. Although still in its infancy, the industry was so profitable that more and more merchant adventurers were drawn into it.

One of the leading patrons of this new industry was the first Lord Spencer, who was also connected with the Washington family. A local tradition says that he aspired to be the owner of 20,000 sheep, but a mortality always attacked his flocks between the 19th and 20th thousand. It was said that once he reached the very odd number of 19,999. It was when the Spencers were raising sheep that Lawrence Washington went into the wool-stapling trade at Northampton, and it may have been largely through his connection with Sir John Spencer that he was enabled to grow rich by buying fleece from the farmers and selling the wool to the manufacturers of Norfolk, Essex, and Yorkshire. He soon became a prominent citizen and was made a member of the corporation while still a young man, and he was chosen mayor in 1632.

Nothing of any note is known of his first mayoralty, but during his second term of office (1545), the corporation had to face an unemployment problem, with heavy taxes and high prices. "In their discretion," as the original entry runs in the book still preserved in the Town Hall, "in order to keep down the price of bread and other necessities, the mayor and corporation enacted that no baker should send into the country more than one horse-load of bread in any one day. No miller, nor person acting for a miller, should go near the market on market day. As it was already illegal to sell corn on market days anywhere except in the market, this was intended to bring the private householder into direct contact with the producer. No person bringing corn into the town should be allowed to keep it from one market day to another. That was to ensure that corn, if there were any, could be purchased at the market value, and could not be kept for a rise." The man who could issue and enforce such rules was no ordinary man.

With such powerful friends as Sir Thomas Kitson, of the Mercers' Company, and Sir John Spencer, with his thousands of sheep, Lawrence Washington, wool stapler, was bound to succeed and acquire wealth very rapidly. Between his two terms as mayor, Lawrence became possessed of the lands of Sulgrave, which had been thrown onto the market by Henry VIII's disruption of the monasteries.

Sulgrave, about fourteen miles southwest of the city of Northampton and six miles northeast of Banbury, was the property of the Priory of St. Andrew of Northampton, at the time of the Dissolution. Lawrence Washington therefore knew all about it, and with such a friend at court as Sir John Spencer no doubt he found little difficulty in obtaining a grant to one of the alienated lands of that religious house. It was also advantageous that the rector of the church at Brington, which the Washingtons attended, was Cromwell's principal commissioner for the dissolution of the monasteries. Thus at a single stroke, Lawrence Washington lifted himself from the simple rank of a tradesman or merchant to that of a squire of the district, although he was well born and probably as well connected by marriage as any of his neighbors. He built himself a handsome house, known as Sulgrave Manor, which has long been considered the ancestral home of the Washington family. Thus he became one of the proud magnates of the county of "spires and squires."

Besides the estate at Sulgrave, Lawrence Washington also acquired at the same time properties at Woodford, Stotesbury, and Cotton, which had also belonged to the priory of St. Andrew. He also acquired certain other lands in Sulgrave, and the belongings of the dissolved priories of Canons Ashby and Gatesby. This transaction took place in 1539, and in 1543 he bought from Sir John Williams and Anthony Stringer a great barn at Stotesbury, no doubt for use in his wool-stapling business.

The old Manor House stands at the east end of the village of Sulgrave. Built of the stone of the district and in the style of the period, it was of a size suitable for persons of the rank and fortune of

Sulgrave Manor, not far from the city of Northampton.

The Great Hall in Sulgrave Manor.

Lawrence Washington. What it was originally, however, and its appearance today are two very different things. Through the centuries, it has undergone many changes and transformations, as well as a few disfigurements.

The house, as it stands, affords a good specimen of the domestic architecture of the 16th and early 17th centuries. It is neither better nor worse than many similar buildings and shows that the builder, even when he decided to provide himself with a house, did not aspire too high. That part of the original structure that remains shows that all the work connected with it was good and substantial, and the adornments of a tasteful though by no means florid character.

Sulgrave Manor, first mentioned in the Domesday Book of 1086, now contains a wealth of interesting souvenirs of the Washingtons in England and America. No visitor to England should miss it.

In 1914, to commemorate a century of peace between Great Britain and the United States, the British Peace Centenary Committee purchased Sulgrave Manor along with ten acres of land, and gave it to the Sulgrave Institution. This organization exists to "bring together in a closer community of interest those societies, associations, and individuals that are engaged in any work which tends toward an understanding of Anglo-Saxon- Celtic culture, laws, and related institutions" and which maintains Sulgrave Manor as a place of pilgrimage for all Americans visiting England, as well as an active center of work for the furtherance of Anglo-American friendship. The restoration and refurnishing were carried out with taste and scholarly care, so that Sulgrave Manor today represents an excellent example of a small manor house and garden at the time of Shakespeare, who was a near neighbor of the Washingtons. The National Society of Colonial Dames of America cooperated with the Sulgrave Manor Board to make sure that the distinctive character and atmosphere were preserved. Every pilgrim who visits this ancient home must feel a deepened sense of the close kinship between the two great English-speaking peoples, to whose mutual friendship the manor is dedicated.

Sulgrave Manor is of significance to Americans because it was the birthplace of the Reverend Lawrence Washington, a great-grandson of the builder, whose son John left England in 1656 to

The kitchen in Sulgrave Manor.

A close-up of the coat-of-arms in Sulgrave Manor.

A bedroom in Sulgrave Manor.

tower, with square buttresses, forms a conspicuous object in the landscape.

Taken as a whole, this church does not rank high in a country famous for structures of this kind. Among the subjects of special interest are the hagioscope, or "squint," enabling persons who were in the south aisle to witness the elevation of the Host. On the south side of the chancel is a small window provided with an oaken shutter, usually known as a "leper's window." On each side of the chancel roof are carved heads, supposedly those of Edward III and his Queen Philippa.

Worthy of note, however, are the old octagonal font and the Norman doorway, with its quaint flower moulding; also, on the south side of the altar, near the floor, the small, square piscina. Equally interesting is the ancient oaken treasure chest of the church, curiously banded with strips of iron. Such oldtime receptacles for records, church plate, vestments, and the like are not uncommon. At one time, such a chest was the hiding place in which a local gang of burglars and highwaymen stored their ill-gotten gains, the parish clerk being an accomplice and covering them and their nefarious proceedings by the screen of his semi-sacred character.

A slab under the east window of the south aisle formerly contained six memorial brasses of the first Lawrence Washington and his family, but what remains of them is very imperfect and much mutilated. The head of the family was represented wearing a close-fitting doublet, a long loose gown bordered with fur and having demi-cannon sleeves and large, broad-toed shoes, the ordinary attire of well-to-do citizens in the days of the Virgin Queen. Fortunately, a drawing of the whole has been preserved, and we can see that the wife appears in a plain costume such as was worn by women of her rank in Tudor times. The four sons and seven daughters of these two were presented in groups on two other brasses. The sons appear in the long doublets and breeches of the period, with long hose and the usual broad-toed shoes, while the girls wore close-fitting caps, with gowns to the ankles, secured by a band around the waist.

The memorial slab was mutilated in August, 1889, by two well dressed individuals who desired admission to the church and who, when gone, were found to have carried away the brasses representing the children.

The plate recording the burial of Lawrence

take up land in Virginia which later became Mt. Vernon.

Sulgrave itself is a typical old English village, situated in the midst of a beautiful and delightfully rural country. It is a short and pleasant drive from the city of Northampton and has long been a favorite pilgrimage for Americans visiting England. In the village itself, the first object of interest is the church, with its solid looking tower at the west end of the village. In the main, it is in the style of architecture known as Decorated, and it dates back to the 14th century. The chancel, with one well preserved window, is of a later period, as is the south porch, dated 1564. The porch on the north side, however, is of the same period as the earlier parts of the building, which consist, in addition to the chancel, of nave and north and south aisles, these being separated from the nave by a Decorated arcade of four bays. Its square, embattled

Washington and his wife Amy does not give the date of Lawrence's death, in 1585, which occurred nineteen years after that of his wife. It has been thought by some that this omission indicates that the trouble which would soon drive the family from Sulgrave was already overshadowing it. Or perhaps there was some lack of business management in Lawrence's eldest son that prevented his having his father's date of death marked on the brass. Care has been taken to preserve this interesting memorial of the Washingtons from further damage or decay, while a reproduction of the original inscription, dating from 1890, has been placed on the wall above it by members of the family.

The Lawrence Washington who built Sulgrave Manor had a large family, but Americans are chiefly interested in his eldest son, Robert, who was a direct ancestor of George Washington. Robert succeeded to the Sulgrave estate on the death of his father, February 19, 1585. He continued in possession until 1610, when, for some reason, probably financial embarrassment, he parted with it to another branch of the family. The exact circumstances are shrouded in mystery. If the problems were financial, they must have developed suddenly, for up until 1610 Robert Washington had maintained his position in the county and had given his sons an education suitable to their station. Christopher and William had gone to Oriel College, Oxford, matriculating in the year of the Spanish Armada, 1588. Christopher graduated with a B.A. degree six years later.

Robert's eldest son was named Lawrence, after his grandfather. With his consent, it was decided to sell Sulgrave to Lawrence Makepeace, a descendant of Lawrence Washington of Northampton through one of his daughters. The manor remained in this family for barely fifty years, thus illustrating the ill luck that is supposed to fall upon those who held alienated church property before the completion of the third generation. It was a strange decline of family fortunes, and may have been one of the immediate causes for the family to emigrate, some forty or fifty years later.

At this unfortunate crisis in the family fortunes, the Spencers proved to be a valuable stay and support. Lawrence Washington, following the lead of his brother Robert, went to live at Brington, close to Althorp, the famous Northamptonshire seat of the Spencer family. In Robert, Lord Spencer, he found a true and constant friend. This old Spencer estate, Althorp, six miles from Northampton, has a superb art collection and is open to the public on Tuesdays, Thursdays, and Sundays, from 2:30 to 6 p.m., from May through September.

The church registers contain the record of the marriage of Robert Washington, the second son of Robert of Sulgrave, and Elizabeth Chishull, which took place on February 19, 1595. The church books also record the baptism of George Washington, a younger son of Lawrence, on August 3, 1608. Apparently both Lawrence and Robert stayed with the Spencers for a season before they moved to Brington. The will of Sir John Spencer, proved on January 11, 1599, bequeaths twenty pounds to Elizabeth Washington, wife of Robert Washington of Great Brington, "in regard to her pains about me in my sickness." It would seem that the relations between the Washingtons and the Spencers were so intimate that Robert Washington's wife practically took charge of the aged knight's sickroom in his last illness. There were no trained nurses in those days, and every woman had to be nurse on occasion.

There were two grandsons of Lawrence Washington (of Northampton and Sulgrave) whose names were associated with the parish of Brington—Lawrence and Robert. After the sale of the Sulgrave estate in 1610, Lawrence retired to Brington, where he died. Great Brington is seven miles northwest of Northampton, and Little Brington is less than a mile south of Great Brington.

The Washington house in Great Brington has no court or garden separating it from the village street. It is a simple structure, with a high-pitched gable, and with certain architectural features that indicate beyond question that it was originally built for a family above the ordinary run of village folk. For example, its four lower windows at the front are mullioned, and there is a square-headed door with moulded dripstone—features not found on any other house in the hamlet. Above the doorway there is a slab bearing an inscription filled with pathos:

> The Lord giveth
> The Lord taketh
> away. Blessed be the
> name of the Lord.
> Constructed
> 1606

The Washington home in Brington.

Inside, the house has been greatly altered to adapt it to modern needs, but the old-fashioned staircases, with sturdy oaken supports, remain as they were when first built. The rooms are low and quaint-looking, the upper ones lighted by small windows close to the eaves. One of the bedrooms shows the old timbers supporting the roof and ceiling. The old beams, oaken floors, panelling, and downstairs cupboards are undoubtedly of early date. At the back of the house, there is a good stretch of garden. There are few villages in the English Midlands more picturesque than Great Brington. The whole country hereabout is undulating, with pleasant views, shaded vales, far-stretching corn lands and meadows, interspersed with well-to-do farmsteads, great houses, and the inevitable church spire for which the county is famous.

The tomb of Lawrence Washington is in the chancel of the church at Brington, and on a stone in the floor of the church may still be seen, with permission of the rector, the Washington coat-of-arms, with those of the wife, and the epitaph. The tomb of Robert Washington and his wife, who

The plaque on the Washington home in Brington.

both died in 1622, is in the nave, with a brass recording above it. In 1861, facsimiles of both memorials were placed in the entrance hall of the Statehouse in Boston, Massachusetts. Robert Washington is thought to have carried on the work of a farmer and a miller. An entry in the Althorp household books shows that he rented a windmill, belonging to Lord Spencer, that was situated about a mile from the village.

Of Lawrence Washington's eight sons and nine daughters, most of the daughters can be traced, but only three of his sons: Sir William Washington of Packington, Sir John Washington of Thrapston, Northants, and the Reverend Lawrence Washington, rector of Purleigh, Essex. It was long thought that Sir John Washington was the emigrant to Virginia, and it was only after research by Colonel Chester had shown the impossibility of this conjecture, that attention became fixed upon that John who was the eldest son of Lawrence who was the Rector of Purleigh. There seems little doubt that this John was the great-grandfather of George Washington.

Lawrence, the brother of Sir William and Sir John, must have been born about 1602, as he matriculated at Brasenose College, Oxford, on November 2, 1621, in his nineteenth year. Two years later he obtained his B.A. degree and in 1626 his M.A. He was Fellow of his college from 1624 to 1633, Lector in 1626, and Proctor in 1631. He finally left the university to take over the rectorship of Purleigh, near Chelmsford, in Essex. Purleigh is situated in the southeastern part of the county, three miles southwest of Maldon. Lawrence Washington was appointed Rector of Purleigh in March, 1632, and held the post until 1643, when he was ejected by order of Parliament as a malignant Royalist. It would seem that his real fault was his fidelity to the royal cause, a fidelity shared with the entire Washington family.

Clergymen in those days found it hard to satisfy all men. What with Protestants on one hand and rigid Puritans on the other, they had to walk very warily, and even then could not be sure of escaping trouble. So high did religious and political feeling run, that overzealous partisans were ever ready to pick holes where none existed and to magnify molehills of faultiness into mountains of error. Many worthy men were deprived of their livings only because their sympathies lay with Cavalier instead of Roundhead, or vice versa.

John Walker, in his *Sufferings of the Clergy* (London, 1714), refers to Reverend Lawrence Washington as "a very worthy, pious man, moder-

The church in Brington, where several of the Washington family are buried.

Fawsley Church, near Sulgrave Manor, where the Washingtons
worshipped.

The window in Fawsley Church showing the Washington coat-of-
arms.

ate and sober" in his life and habits. According to those who knew him well, he was a loyal person. The charges brought against him were held to be proved, and he was dismissed in early 1643 after ten years of service among his parishioners, and he suffered a good deal in consequence. Later he was given a small living in the same district. Little is known of his subsequent life, spent mostly at or near Tring, in Hertfordshire. Three of his children were born in Tring.

The oldest son, John, emigrated to Virginia some time between 1655 and 1657, when he was about twenty-four years old. Lawrence was married to Mary Jones on June 26, 1660, at Luton, about twelve miles from Tring. In December, 1663, their daughter Mary was baptized at the same place. It was therefore sometime after 1663, probably in 1666, that Lawrence Washington and his family emigrated to Virginia.

When these young Washingtons pulled up stakes in England, it had become common, if not fashionable, for younger and poorer members of noble and aristocratic families, seeing things so much against them in their native land, to cast in their lot with the pioneers of the wilderness. Many friends of the young Washingtons had already gone to America and others were planning to go. They had a powerful friend in Sir Edwin Sandys (son of Dr. Edwin Sandys, Archbishop of York), who was treasurer of the Virginia Company, and with whose family there was a Washington connection.

Most of those who chose to go out to Virginia did so for the sake of finding a home and a career, and there is no reason to suppose that the Washingtons had any other motive for going, unless the recollection of the treatment their father had received at the hands of the Puritans for his loyalty to the King or from his family connections because of his marriage, rankled in their bosoms. Not a few chose exile in the hope of enjoying greater freedom of worship in the new land.

John Washington, the first of the family to emigrate, had a son named Lawrence, who married Mildred Warner. They in turn had a son named Augustine, who became a wealthy landowner in Virginia. Augustine first married Jane Butler, by whom he had four children, and later married Mary Ball, who had six children, of whom the first became America's first president. George Washington was born at Bridges Creek, Westmoreland

The statue of George Washington on Trafalgar Square, London.

County, Virginia, on February 22, 1732. Thus it was George Washington's great-grandfather, John Washington, who founded the Washington family in America.

Augustine Washington died when young George was only eleven, so the boy divided his time between the home of his half-brother Lawrence, at Mt. Vernon, and his own old home, Bridges Farm, where lived his other half-brother, Augustine. His mother, Mary Ball Washington, died in 1789.

In addition to the showplaces of Washington Old Hall, Sulgrave Manor, and the Church of St. Mary the Virgin at Great Brington, there are numerous memorials to George Washington or his ancestors in many parts of England.

In the 700-year-old church at Fawsley, near Daventry, in Northamptonshire, there are six windows with heraldic shields showing the coat-of-arms of the various families who married into the Washington families. These were brought from

Sulgrave in 1830. The church has many other interesting features, such as the mural monuments, some of the finest in Britain; the carvings on the 16th century pews; and the moat which surrounds the church.

The church and manor house at Garsdon, near Malmesbury, Wiltshire, have ancestral links with George Washington, and five members of the family are buried here. In this church there is a monument to Rev. Lawrence Washington, who died in 1643, which was restored in 1906 by Bishop Potter of New York.

Other church memorials to the Washingtons are found in a number of villages: Steeple, near Wareham, Dorset; Thrapston, near Kettering, Northamptonshire; Tring, Herefordshire; and in All Saints Church, in Maidstone, Kent. In the Royal West of England Academy, in Bristol, there are portraits of George Washington and other leaders in the War of Independence.

In London, there are several memorials to the first American President, including a small bronze bust in the crypt of St. Paul's Cathedral and a statue outside the National Portrait Gallery, on the north side of Trafalgar Square, which was a gift of the people of Virginia. There is a portrait of George Washington at 10 Downing Street, the official residence of the Prime Minister, while in the British Museum there is a letter from him, dated 1793, regarding a plan for the new city of Washington, D.C.

10

Benjamin Franklin

There is no question about Benjamin Franklin's ancestry or descent. Like Washington, he was descended from a Northamptonshire family. The Franklins had long been established in the county when an offshoot detached himself from the parent flock, crossed the Atlantic, and took root on the American continent.

Franklin's father was a native of Ecton, where the Franklins had been established for three hundred years and probably much longer. Members of that sturdy class known as yeomen, they enjoyed a patrimony of thirty acres. In addition to cultivating the land, Franklin's father carried on a blacksmith's business, thus considerably augmenting the family resources. For generations, the eldest son had been brought up in this trade, which in those days was a vitally important one.

The first of the Franklins of whom there is any record was one Henry Franklin, whose son Thomas was baptized at Ecton Church on October 8, 1598. This Thomas became a man of some importance in the village counsels. He was acting churchwarden in 1653, when a collection was made in the village for the relief of the townsfolk of Marlborough, Wiltshire, and he signed the register in confirmation of that fact on September 6 of that year. According to his son Josiah, Thomas Franklin was "imprisoned for a year and a day on suspicion of being the author of some poetry that touched the character of some great man." This points to a literary gift that apparently ran in the family and cropped out again in his grandson Benjamin.

This rural Thomas the Rhymer had four sons, of whom the eldest, also named Thomas, was baptized at Ecton in 1637 and died there on January 6, 1702. The second son, John, became a wool-dyer and settled in Banbury, while Benjamin, the third, emigrated to America and died there at an advanced age. The fourth and youngest son, Josiah, served an apprenticeship to his brother John, and then emigrated to America in 1685, after he was married and had three children. In America, he had four more children, and when his first wife died, he married again and had ten more, making a total of seventeen. The American Benjamin Franklin was the youngest of the ten boys in this large family.

Of the four sons of Thomas the Rhymer, Thomas seems to have been the most important. Although learned in the art of blacksmith and, according to some, in bell-founding, which was apparently practiced by the Franklins, he did not confine himself to these crafts, but took to book-learning and qualified as a scrivener, attaining more than local repute in the county. He became clerk to the Commissioners of Taxes, and it may have been in this capacity, or something similar, that he made the acquaintance of Lord Halifax, who became his friend and patron.

In a letter written from London after his visit to Ecton in 1768, Benjamin Franklin says of this uncle: "He was a conveyancer, something of a lawyer, clerk of the county courts, and clerk to the Archdeacon in his visitations. He set on foot a subscription for erecting chimes in the steeple of

The church at Ecton, where the Franklin family had lived for three hundred years.

the parish church, and effected his purpose. And we heard them play the same old airs, 'Britons, Strike Home' and a hymn tune.'' More important, and quite in the style of his famous nephew, was Thomas Franklin's discovery of a method whereby their village meadows could be saved from flooding when the river Nene overflowed. No one could conceive how it could be done, but the townspeople knew that if Thomas Franklin said he could, it would be done. These and other examples of his uncle's accomplishments and character were related to Benjamin Franklin and his son by the wife of the village rector.

Thomas Franklin's gravestone may be seen today in Ecton churchyard, with the inscription, "Here lyeth the body of Thomas Franklin, who departed this life January 6th, Anno Dei. 1702 in the sixty-fifth year of his age." His widow survived him some nine years, dying on March 14, 1711, at the age of seventy-seven.

There was nothing in the Ecton church, however, to mark the association with the family of the

world-famous Benjamin Franklin until 1910, when a group of Americans provided a bronze tablet with a bust in relief of their great countryman, and this quotation from one of his speeches, "The longer I live, the more convincing proof I see of this truth, that God governs in the affairs of men."

It is characteristic of these Franklins that they were strong Protestants, and during Queen Mary's reign ran some danger of persecution on account of their hostility to the ancient faith. In his *Autobiography* Benjamin Franklin tells how he learned from his uncle that in the perilous days of Mary, the family concealed their English Bible by means of tapes under and within the cover of a joint-stool. When his great-grandfather wished to read it to his family, he placed the joint-stool on his knees and then turned over the leaves under the tapes. One of the children stood at the door to give notice if he saw an officer of the spiritual court coming that way, in which case the stool was turned down upon its feet and the Bible concealed as before.

The Franklins appear to have steered clear of

ecclesiastical molestation until the house of Protestantism became divided against itself, when some of the ministers ejected for their non-conformity held meetings in the neighborhood. Benjamin and Josiah became innoculated with the views that were taught and remained true to them all their lives. It appears that their dissent led eventually to the two brothers' migration to America. Certainly this was true of the younger, Josiah, who was the father of the American Benjamin Franklin. "The venticles being at the time forbidden by law," says his son, "and frequently disturbed in the meetings, some considerable men of his acquaintance determined to go to that country, and he was prevailed upon to accompany them thither, where they expected to enjoy the exercise of their religion with freedom."

Benjamin Franklin describes his father, born at Ecton in 1698, as a man of sound sense and independant character, strong in his views on political and religious matters. Though precluded by his large family and straitened circumstances from taking part in public affairs, he was frequently consulted by leading citizens as to his opinion on matters of public interest and those of the church to which he belonged. He took special pains in bringing up his children, of whom he reared thirteen out of seventeen. As often as possible, he would invite some friend or neighbor to his home and engage them in some useful topic of conversation, so that the minds of the children would be stimulated and improved by listening to their discussions. He was also something of a draughtsman, had some skill in music, and in the evening would sing very pleasantly, accompanying himself on the violin. His first wife was Jane White of Banbury, and his second was a daughter of Peter Folger, an Englishman from Norwich who became one of the first settlers of Waterton, Massachusetts. Mr. Folger was a man of exceptional character and some literary talent, which Benjamin Franklin may have inherited, along with some facial characteristics similar to those of the Folger family.

Benjamin, the other brother who emigrated to America, was equally gifted in his way. His famous nephew considered him too much of a politician for a man who was only a silk dyer and felt that this might have militated against his success in life. Nevertheless, he was an ingenious man, a great reader, and, like his father, addicted to poetry. One gathers that he had not a little influence on his godson, whom he taught a system of shorthand that he had invented. It is also possible that he turned young Ben's attention to literary matters.

Of the second brother, John, who settled at Banbury, less is known than of the others. He seems to have been a man of intelligence and estimable character. The father, Thomas the Rhymer, went to live with John in his declining years. He left the Ecton house, with the land, to his oldest son, Thomas, who in turn bequeathed the estate to his only daughter. Benjamin Franklin records having seen his Uncle John's gravestone in Banbury in 1758.

When Benjamin Franklin visited his ancestral village in 1758, there appears to have been no one of the Franklin name left in Ecton. After hundreds of years of residence, the last member of the family had gone. There is a street named Franklin's Close, however, and in the church at Ecton there is a modern memorial to Benjamin Franklin, and his uncle and aunt are buried in the churchyard.

Today the reflected light from Benjamin Franklin's personality and achievements illumines the little village where his forefathers lived and toiled for so many generations, possibly even from Saxon times, when the name they bore stood for a class of freeholders above the free tenants. In other words, the "Frenkelein" (as in Chaucer) was distinguished from other freeholders by the extent of his possessions. Benjamin Franklin was proud of his ancestors, proud to have descended from so respectable and worthy a stock, and it is no small test of a family's strength and virility to have been able to maintain its grip on the same home and holding for hundreds of years. When in England, Franklin took great pains to find out all he could about his forebears and their home in Ecton.

Ecton is a quiet little village, four or five miles northeast of Northampton, on the high ground overlooking the valley of the river Nene, with many interesting places near by. Earls Barton, with its fine old church, is notable as showing vestiges of Anglo-Saxon work; Castle Ashby is one of the beautiful homes of the Earls of Northampton; Yardley Chase, Easton Maudit, was long the residence of Percy (of the *Reliques of Ancient English Poetry*) before he became Bishop of Dromore.

Although so intimately associated with the Franklins, Ecton today has no house clearly definable as their dwelling place. When Benjamin

A street in Ecton named after the Franklin family.

Franklin was there, in 1758, the house was still standing, "a decayed old stone building," even then known as the Franklin House and occupied by a person who kept a school. Tradition says it was destroyed by fire. In a garden adjoining the rectory, there was a well known as Franklin's Well, and it is thought that the Franklin smithy may have stood at this spot, since it is near the main street of the village. It is possible that the manor house became the home of the last Franklins to live in Ecton. Certainly Thomas, the scrivener, could hardly have continued to work as a blacksmith while holding the offices he did; it is not at all unlikely that he gave up the smithy, and the house connected with it, and found the manor house more convenient and suitable to his dignity as a county official.

In those days, Ecton was noted for the number of Hogarth paintings it could show. The artist frequently visited his friend, Mr. Whalley, the rector at Ecton, and did much of his painting there. Several of his paintings were in the rectory, and Mr. Isted, lord of the manor, possessed others.

Born on January 7, 1706, Benjamin Franklin grew up in a modest home in Boston, where his eager mind and strong body were molded by his earnest parents according to the precepts of their Puritan faith. Franklin's mother, Abiah Folger, was the daughter of one of the pioneer settlers of the island of Nantucket. She was a deeply religious woman and termed by her son "a discreet and virtuous woman." Young Franklin soon became a leader among the neighborhood children, but he spent less than two years in formal schooling before he was pressed into his father's trade—candle- and soap-making.

Although young Benjamin had great mechanical aptitude, like his father, it was soon obvious that his greatest talents were intellectual. He devoured the books in his father's library, again and again reading Bunyan's *Pilgrims Progress,* Plutarch's *Lives,* Daniel Defoe's *Essay on Projects,* and Cotton Mather's *Essays to Do Good.* From these books, Franklin gained the precepts that guided him throughout life, namely, that life was purposeful and should be lived in service to God and man, that by acting together men could make the world better, and that England was a great and powerful nation because she had been righteous and enterprising.

Intrigued by words, Franklin became a printer's apprentice under his half-brother James, who had founded the *New England Courant* in 1721. When he was only sixteen, young Benjamin burst into print with some satirical letters signed "Mistress Silence Dogood." He slipped the letters under the door of the printing house at night, so that his brother would not know who had written them. It was generally agreed, however, that they were *not* written by a woman, despite the signature. In these pieces young Franklin attacked the pomposity and narrow-mindedness of officialdom. A year later, James Franklin was jailed for a month for having suggested anti-government ideas in his paper. In order to continue publication, he put Benjamin in charge of the *Courant.* After reading Joseph Addison's *Spectator* papers, young Benjamin drew up his own rules for good writing. He said that "Good writing ought to have a tendency to benefit the reader, by improving his virtue and his knowledge . . . it should proceed regularly from things known to things unknown, distinctly and clearly without confusion. The words used should be the most expressive the language affords, provided they are the most generally understood. Nothing should be expressed in two words that can be as well expressed in one . . . the whole should be as short as possible, consistent with clearness. The words should be so placed as to be agreeable to the ear in reading; summarily, it should be smooth, clear, and short."

Franklin was ambitious to be more than his brother's helper, so at the age of seventeen he went to Philadelphia, where he found a job with a printer named Samuel Keimer. The next year he was on his way to England with promises of aid to purchase his own printing equipment.

The young man sailed on the *London Hope,* arriving at Gravesend, Kent, on Christmas Eve, 1724, with his friend James Ralph, also from Philadelphia. The two then made their way to London and found lodgings in Little Britain Street, not far from St. Paul's. Young Franklin soon had a job at a famous printing house in Bartholomew Close. The Church of St. Bartholomew-the-Great in West Smithfield, London EC 1, was part of a great Augustinian Priory founded in 1123 by Rahere, a favorite of Henry I. The Lady Chapel, behind the Choir, was used as a printing works by a man called Palmer, for whom Franklin worked. James Ralph eventually became a partner of Henry Fielding, and together they opened the Little Theatre in Haymarket, in 1735.

Franklin worked for Palmer for a year. "I was pretty diligent," he says in his *Autobiography,* "but I spent with Ralph a good deal of my earnings at plays and public amusements." When Franklin found that he disagreed with some of the reasoning in Wollaston's *Religion of Nature,* for which he was setting the type, he wrote a little metaphysical piece and printed a small number. His employer, Mr. Palmer, admired the young man's ingenuity, though he disagreed with his reasoning.

When Franklin found a good second-hand bookstore next to his lodgings in Little Britain, he arranged to take, read, and return any of the books, upon very satisfactory financial terms. This was before the days of circulating libraries, so Franklin was elated at his deal. In later years, he started the first lending library in America.

A printing press from Lincoln's Inn Fields, similar to that which Franklin used.

The ancient ruins of Stonehenge, in southern England, which Franklin visited in 1757.

Franklin's pamphlet came to the notice of a surgeon named Lyons, who came to see the young author and took him to an alehouse in Cheapside and later to Batson's Coffeehouse, where he met many congenial people. When Sir Hans Sloane heard of an asbestos purse, which purifies by fire, that Franklin had brought from America, he came to see the young man and invited him to his home in Bloomsbury Square.

After a year, Franklin left Palmer's to work at Watts's, near Lincoln's Inn Fields, a still greater printing house. He stayed at Watts until his return to America in 1726. When he changed jobs, he also changed his living quarters, for Little Britain was too far away from the printing house, so he found lodgings in Duke's Court, on Sardinia Street (WC 2), opposite the Romish Chapel. While working at Watts, he met a wealthy young man named Wyngate, who had been better educated than most printers. Franklin taught young Wyngate and a friend of his to swim. On one occasion, a group challenged Franklin to perform, so he stripped off his clothes and leaped into the Thames, swimming from near Chelsea to Blackfriars, performing many stunts along the way, both upon and under the water, that surprised and pleased the spectators.

On another occasion, Franklin demonstrated, in a reservoir in Green Park, the principle of pouring oil on troubled waters.

When his friend Mr. Denham made young Franklin an offer to work in his mercantile business in Philadelphia, Franklin accepted and took leave of printing, as he thought, forever. After eighteen months in London, he sailed on the *Berkshire* on July 23, 1726, from Gravesend, arriving in Philadelphia on October 11.

Franklin had been religiously brought up as a Presbyterian, but he seldom attended any public worship. Imbued with a strong sense of moral principles, however, he drew up his own list of virtues, as follows, with the intention of acquiring the habitude of all these virtues:

1. Temperance. Eat not to dullness; drink not to elevation.
2. Silence. Speak not but what may benefit others or yourself; avoid trifling conversation.
3. Order. Let all your things have their places; let each part of your business have its time.

4. Resolution. Resolve to perform what you ought; perform without fail what you resolve.
5. Frugality. Make no expense but to do good to others or yourself; that is, waste nothing.
6. Industry. Lose no time; be always employed in something useful; cut off all unnecessary actions.
7. Sincerity. Use no hurtful deceit; think innocently and justly; and, if you speak, speak accordingly.
8. Justice: Wrong none by doing injuries, or omitting the benefits that are your duty.
9. Moderation. Avoid extremes; forbear resenting injuries so much as you think they deserve.
10. Cleanliness. Tolerate no uncleanliness in body, clothes, or habitation.
11. Tranquility. Be not disturbed at trifles, or at accidents common or unavoidable.
12. Chastity.
13. Humility. Imitate Jesus and Socrates.

A few years later, in 1732, Franklin published his first *Almanac,* under the name of Richard Saunders. Later he changed the name to *Poor Richard's Almanac* and continued to publish it for twenty-five years. As he said, "I endeavored to make it both entertaining and useful, and it accordingly came to be in such demand that I reaped considerable profit from it, vending annually near ten thousand."

Besides writing and publishing, Franklin was busy inventing and patenting many useful devices, including an open stove, "for the better warming of rooms, and at the same time saving fuel, as the fresh air admitted was warmed in entering." Many of his inventions were patented by others, who made a great profit from them, but Franklin never contested the matter, "having no desire of profiting by patents myself, and hating disputes."

In 1753, Franklin was appointed postmaster-general of America, by the postmaster-general of England. Under Franklin's guidance, the post office service and general management were vastly improved, but at great initial expense. During the first four years, the post office ran up a debt of nine hundred pounds. After that, however, the improvements began to pay off, and soon the American post office was bringing in three times as much clear revenue to the Crown as the post office of Ireland.

While on post-office business, Franklin made a trip to New England, where the College of Cambridge presented him with a Master of Arts degree. Yale College had previously paid him a similar compliment. As he says, "Thus, without studying in any college, I came to partake of their honors. They were conferred in consideration of my improvements and discoveries in the electric branch of natural philosophy."

Franklin returned to England in 1757, landing at Falmouth, Cornwall, on July 17. After arriving in England, Franklin says, "I set out immediately, with my son, for London, and we only stopped a little by the way to view Stonehenge on Salisbury Plain, and Lord Pembroke's house and gardens, with very curious antiquities, at Wilton. We arrived in London the 27th of July, 1757."

This time he found lodgings at No. 7 Craven Street (now No. 36) in the house of Mrs. Margaret Stevenson, and they "proved so convenient, comfortable, and in every way pleasant" that he made his home there during all his long subsequent residence in London. Craven Street is now next to Charing Cross station, but in Franklin's day, Hungerford Market adjoined this street.

By this time, Franklin had achieved a world-wide reputation as a writer, scientist, and inventor. He had also served for several years as a member of the Pennsylvania Assembly. By 1757, he was the foremost British patriot in the United States and also the leading defender of American rights.

During this second trip to England, Franklin enjoyed the friendship of the most learned men in the British Isles and visited in the most cultivated circles. He wrote that "I seldom dine at home in winter, and could spend the whole summer in the country houses of inviting friends, if I chose it." Except for the years 1762-64, spent in Pennsylvania amid renewed Indian and political warfare, Franklin lived for eighteen years the life of an intellectual gentleman at the center of the British Empire. He often met with his friends at the Pennsylvania Coffeehouse in Birchin Lane, or at the London Coffee House, 42 Ludgate Hill, where he was a member.

While he was living in Craven Street, Lord Chatham called upon Franklin, in 1758, in order to get his views upon the all-important subjects that were beginning to cause trouble between the Colonies and the mother country. Also from these quarters he wrote, in 1760, to Lord Kames relative to the portrait of William Penn, which his lordship had offered Franklin: "Were it certainly his portrait," wrote Franklin, "it would be too valuable a curiosity for me to think of accepting it. I should only desire to take a copy of it. I could wish to know the history of the picture before it came into your hands, and the grounds for supposing it his. I have at present grave doubts about it, first, because the primitive Quakers declared against pictures as a vain expense; a man's suffering his portrait to be taken was conceived as pride; and I think to this day it is very little practiced among them. Then it is on a board; and I imagine the practice of painting on boards did not come down so low as Penn's times; but of this I am not certain. My other reason is an anecdote I have heard, viz., that when old Lord Cobham was adorning his gardens at Stowe with busts of famous men, he made inquiry of the family for a picture of William Penn in order to get a bust formed from it, but could find none; that Sylvanus Bevan—the old Quaker apothecary, remarkable for the notice he takes of countenances and a knack he has of cutting in ivory strong likenesses of persons he has once seen—hearing of Lord Cobham's desire, set himself to recollect Penn's face, with which he had been well acquainted, and cut a little bust of him in ivory, which he sent to Lord Cobham, without any letter of notice that it was Penn's. But my lord, who had personally known Penn, on seeing it immediately cried out, 'Whence comes this? It is William Penn himself!' And from the little bust, they say, the larger one in the gardens was found."

In England, Franklin was increasingly occupied with the relationship between the colonies and the mother country. He believed that their interests were complementary and that by being united, Englishmen on both sides of the Atlantic could enjoy greater liberty and prosperity. After the Stamp Act crisis, however, Franklin expressed strong forebodings: "America, an immense territory, favored by Nature . . . , must become a great country, populous and mighty . . . the seeds of liberty are universally found there, and nothing can eradicate them. And yet, there remains among that people so much respect, veneration, and affection for Britain, that, if cultivated prudently they might be easily governed still for ages, without force, nor

any considerable expense. But I do not see in England a sufficient quantity of the wisdom that is necessary . . . and I lament the want of it . . . Every act of oppression will sour American tempers."

Franklin would frequently stay with Lord Kames in Blair Drummond, Perthshire, and there he planted some trees which still flourish. He also visited often at Twyford House, in Winchester, the home of Dr. Shipley, and he wrote some of his *Autobiography* there.

Franklin's deep commitment to the way of life he knew in America, as well as the corruption and contempt he encountered in British ruling circles, doomed his efforts. On January 29, 1774, he was brought before the Privy Council at Whitehall and accused of stealing letters from Thomas Hutchinson, the hated governor of Massachusetts. For a full hour and a half he stood silently in the cockpit, refusing to dignify the accusations by a single word in his own defense. He was dismissed from his office as postmaster and vilified in the British press as an "old snake" and "an old veteran of mischief." After this public abuse, Franklin returned to America in disgust, sailing from Portsmouth on the *Pennsylvania Packet* on March 25, 1775. Thus at the age of sixty-nine he returned to his native land to take up his role in the forefront of the Revolution.

Thus committed to independence, Franklin took a seat in the Continental Congress and worked diligently to prepare for the war he thought sure to come. At the age of seventy he served on the committee to draft the Declaration of Independence, took a perilous though unsuccessful trip to Montreal to try to persuade Canada to join the revolt, helped to draft Pennsylvania's first state constitution, and proposed a plan of union for the thirteen colonies.

Finally, at the end of 1776, Franklin went to France to seek money and supplies for the American army. During his nine years in France, he was received with acclaim and affection by all groups—patriotic, military, royal, and intellectual. He became a close friend of Voltaire, and at the same time he was beloved by the servant class.

Franklin's notable experiments and discoveries with electricity had been more or less ignored in England until attention was called to the acclaim he had received on the Continent, especially in France. As he says, "Without my having made any application for that honor, they chose me a member of the Royal Society and voted that I should be excused the customary payments, which would have amounted to twenty-five guineas; and ever since have given me their *Transactions* gratis. They also presented me with the gold medal of Sir Godfrey Copley for the year 1753, the delivery of which was accompanied by a very handsome speech of the president, Lord Macclesfield, wherein I was highly honored."

Other honors also came his way. He was made a Freeman of the city of Edinburgh in 1768. He set up the first lightning conductors at Cooper Hall, in 1770, near Walton-le-Dale, Preston, Lancastershire. As a member of a committee of the Royal Society, Franklin advised that such conductors should be placed on Buckingham Palace, which was then done.

From a humble journeyman printer, Benjamin Franklin rose by his own ability and achievement to be a fellow of the Royal Society, to win the highest academic distinctions in the universities of Oxford, Edinburgh, and St. Andrews, and to hold high and important offices in connection with the newly formed American nation, for which his wisdom had done so much in helping to pilot it through troubled and dangerous waters into the haven of safety. Benjamin Franklin died on April 17, 1790, at the age of eighty-four.

Franklin's lodgings on Craven Street, London.

11

John Adams and Later Presidents

Just a few miles from Ecton and a short distance from Sulgrave Manor is the charming village of Flore, the ancestral seat of the Adams family. It must have been fragrant with flowers long before William the Conqueror, for it is listed in his Domesday Book. There is a charming, thatched-roof cottage in Flore that has long been considered the home of John Adams' ancestors. It lies up a small alleyway opposite a row of new bungalows in Kings Lane. The village lies in a gentle slope that leads down to the river Nene, and the church stands by a gabled and pinnacled Elizabethan manor house at one end of the village. Thus we see that three of the most influential families in early America—the Washingtons, the Franklins, and the Adamses—all came from the same small area in England.

John Adams was born in Braintree (now Quincy), Massachusetts, in 1735. He was the son of John Adams, a substantial farmer, and Susannah Bolyston, the daughter of a prominent British family. As a lawyer and effective writer on theories of government, Adams played an active role in drawing up the Declaration of Independence and in the Revolution itself.

During the debates over the adoption of the Declaration of Independence, Adams made a fiery speech on the floor of the Second Continental Congress, convened at Independence Hall in 1776. This stirring oration turned the tide of the debate and helped to bring about the unanimous adoption of the Declaration that gave our nation birth. Mr. Adams ended his oration with these lines:

Through the thick gloom of the present, I see the brightness of the future, as the sun in heaven. We shall make this a glorious, an immortal day. When we are in our graves, our children will honor it. They will celebrate it with thanks-giving, with festivity, with bonfires, and illuminations. On its annual return, they will shed tears, not of subjection and slavery, not of agony and distress, but of gratitude and of joy.

Sir, before God, I believe the hour is come. My judgment approves this measure and my whole heart is in it. All that I have, and all that I am, and all that I hope in this life, I am now ready here to stake upon it. And—I leave off as I began, that live or die, survive or perish, I am for the Declaration. It is my living sentiment, and by the blessing of ‚God, it shall be my dying sentiment: Independence now and Independence forever!

Adams was appointed by Congress as Minister to negotiate treaties of peace and commerce with Great Britain. In Paris, he joined with Franklin and Jay in negotiations with the British commissioners, which terminated in the Treaty of 1783, ending the Revolutionary War.

In 1785, John Adams became the first American Minister to the Court of St. James, but he was unable to work out favorable trade agreements with the British. While in England, however, Adams wrote his *Defense of the Constitution in the United States.* He returned to America in time to be elected vice-president in Washington's new administration, holding that office for two terms and helping the President to establish the traditions

The ancestral Adams home in Flore.

John Adams's home in London, at 9 Grosvenor Square.

All Hallows Church, in London, where John Adams married Louisa Johnson.

In 1781, he served in St. Petersburg as secretary to Francis Dana, the American plenipotentiary to Russia. Two years later he was in Paris as his father's secretary, when John Adams was helping to negotiate peace with Britain.

In 1785, John Quincy Adams returned to the U.S. and studied at Harvard and then read law and was admitted to the bar in 1790. Like his father, he was more interested in politics than law, and he soon came to the attention of President Washington. He was appointed Minister to The Netherlands, and then served briefly in England and later in Berlin. While in London, he married Louisa Catherine Johnson, daughter of the American consul in London.

Louisa Johnson was born on February 12, 1775, in London, where her father, Joshua Johnson of Maryland, was then in business. Since the Johnson family took the American side during the Revolution, Mr. Johnson thought it wise to move to Nantes, in France, rather than to remain in Britain. While living in France, Louisa learned to speak French without an accent.

When the war ended, Joshua Johnson returned to London, where he served as consul until 1797. In 1794, when she was nineteen years old, Louisa Johnson met John Quincy Adams, who immediately fell in love with her. They became engaged and were married on July 26, 1797, at All Hallows Church in London. This is the same church in which William Penn was baptized, on October 23, 1644.

All Hallows Barking by the Tower was founded as early as 675, but was largely rebuilt in the 13th to the 15th centuries. After severe war damage in 1940, the north aisle was reopened for service in 1949. The name "Barking" refers to the early possession of the church by the Abbey of Barking, in Essex. From the brick tower, erected in 1658, Samuel Pepys viewed the devastation caused by the Great Fire of 1666. The work of restoration was completed in 1957, and in 1959, a handsome steeple was added.

At the time of the wedding, Mr. Adams was planning to go to Lisbon, as Minister to Portugal, but his orders were changed and he was sent to Berlin. The young couple lived in the German capital for four years and made many strong social ties.

In 1801, John Quincy Adams returned to America, where he was elected to the Senate. He

of the new government. In 1796, he succeeded Washington as the second American president. In the 1800 election, Adams was defeated by Jefferson, and he retired to Braintree (now Quincy), where he spent twenty-five years on his farm. Along with Washington, Jefferson, and Madison, Adams stands among the greatest of the Founding Fathers.

John Adams lived to be ninety years old, and saw his son, John Quincy Adams, become the sixth president of the United States. John Adams died on July 4, 1826, exactly fifty years after the signing of the Declaration of Independence.

John Adams' eldest son, John Quincy Adams, was born in 1767. He had little formal schooling, but made up for this deficiency by extensive travel abroad and study at various European academies.

resigned this seat, however, and was appointed Minister to Russia by President Madison in 1809. Although neither Mr. nor Mrs. Adams enjoyed St. Petersburg, they lived there until April, 1814, when Mr. Adams was named one of the commissioners to negotiate for peace with Britain, after the War of 1812.

Because of the confusion in Europe and the rigors of such a long and tiring journey, it was decided that Mrs. Adams would remain in St. Petersburg, while her husband journeyed to Ghent to serve on the peace commission. The next few months were excessively trying, because she disliked the Russian capital and was alone with her son, young Charles Francis Adams, who was only six. The worst part was that she could make no plans for the future. Her health was delicate and she shrank from responsibility. Somewhat to Mr. Adams's surprise, the peace treaty was signed on December 24, 1814, and he immediately wrote his wife and asked her to leave Russia, and to meet him in Paris. From there they went to London, where John Quincy Adams served as American Minister to Great Britain.

Before his marriage, Adams had lived at 9 Grosvenor Square, where a plaque now marks the house. Later he lived in a house on Duke Street, at the corner of Brook Street, until 1788. When he and Mrs. Adams and their son returned to London in 1815, they lived in Ealing, in west London, and his children attended school in that area. Adams' sister, Mrs. Van Wart, had a house in Birmingham, Warwickshire, and he often stayed there, calling it "my English home."

John Quincy Adams had another tie with England which greatly benefited America, but which few Americans know about. When James Smithson, an Englishman who had never been in America, willed half a million dollars to build a museum in the United States, some Americans thought he was crazy. Congress debated the offer for ten years, but finally accepted it, after continuous pressure from John Quincy Adams. Today the Smithsonian Institution is the largest museum-gallery complex in the world, occupying thirteen buildings in the heart of Washington, D.C., and housing a collection of antiques and art valued at more than ninety million dollars.

Other than the plaque on the house in Grosvenor Square, there seem to be no memorials in England to John Adams or to his son, John Quincy Adams. Possibly the feeling against them ran too high, because of their strong advocacy of independence for the colonies, and the British were not in a mood to perpetuate the name.

Considering that the American colonies were primarily settled by people from Britain, it is not surprising that most of the early presidents, and even some of the more recent ones, had close ancestral links with the United Kingdom. In several cases, the ancestral homes are still standing.

The home of William Arthur, father of President Chester Alan Arthur, may still be seen at Cullybackey, in County Antrim, Ireland. Antrim is the most northeasterly county of Northern Ireland and is also one of the most scenic. After attending college in Belfast, the elder Arthur emigrated to America, where he married.

James Buchanan's grandparents, John and Jane Russell, were also early emigrants from Northern Ireland, coming from County Tyrone.

Ulysses S. Grant's ancestral home at Dergina, near Ballygawley, County Tyrone, is still standing.

Andrew Jackson's family had settled in County Antrim in Cromwellian days. His great-grandfather, Isaac, married Anne Evans and they had three sons and lived in Carrickfergus. Of the three, Hugh Jackson lived nearby at Boneybefore, in County Antrim. He had four sons, one of whom, Andrew, sailed to America in 1765 with his wife and their two children. He died two years later, but five days before his death, his son Andrew was born, who became the seventh president of the United States.

James Monroe's ancestors are said to go back to Ocaan, Prince of Fermanagh, in the year 1000. A descendant lived on the mount near the river Roe, hence the name Mountroe, or Monroe. The fifth American president was a direct descendant of the fourteenth Baron Foulis, whose son David married a close relative, Agnes Monroe. Their son, Andrew, was captured in the Battle of Preston and banished to Virginia, where he founded the American branch of the family.

On his father's side, William McKinley was descended from a County Antrim family who owned Conagher's Farm, near Dervock, in County Tyrone. The president's great-great-grandfather emigrated to America in 1743. In the early days the name was spelled McKinlay.

James Polk's ancestors came from Londonderry, a county adjoining Antrim.

Woodrow Wilson's grandfather, James Wilson,

worked at a printing works in Strabane, County Tyrone, Northern Ireland, and emigrated to America in 1807. The ancestral home at Dergalt, County Tyrone, is still standing. The president's mother was born in Carlisle, Cumberland, England.

County Wexford, bordering on the Irish Sea, was the ancestral home of John F. Kennedy, and a park has been built in this county in his honor. Situated about 120 miles southeast of Dublin, the park is located about four miles south of New Ross, the town generally described as Kennedy's ancestral home. Dedicated in 1968, the park was financed by Irish-American societies in the United States and is now being developed and operated by the Irish government as the country's only arboretum. More than 3,000 types of trees and shrubs from all over the world have been planted, and eventually 6,000 species will be represented. The park buildings were designed by Irish architects and are built of Irish materials: Liscannor stone from County Clare and Connemara marble flooring. There is a fountain made of Irish granite on which are inscribed the memorable words of the late President: "Ask not what your country can do for you. . . ask what you can do for your country."

Directly south of the park and near the village of Dunganstown is the Kennedy homestead, a modest group of whitewashed stone buildings still occupied by a Kennedy cousin, the elderly Mrs. Mary Ryan. Her two daughters live at the homestead and welcome the many visitors who come from America. In a small building just inside the gate there are two cards, one of which states that "President Kennedy visited this house as Congress-

man in 1947 and as President of the United States on June 27, 1963," and the other, "This small building is part of the old Kennedy home where President Kennedy's great-grandfather was born in 1820. Only part of the walls of the original house, which was a long thatched one containing four or five rooms, still remain. The present house was built in 1870."

There are several other memorials to Kennedy in Britain, one at Runnymede (see chapter seventeen) and one in London. In front of the International Students House, on Park Crescent, London, a memorial bust of John F. Kennedy was placed in 1965. Another memorial consists of scholarships, which enable young men and women from Britain to spend an academic year at Harvard, Radcliffe, or the Massachusetts Institute of Technology.

Abraham Lincoln was of English descent on both sides of his family. His father was descended from Samuel Lincoln, who came to Massachusetts from England in 1637. His mother's people, the Hanks family, came from Malmsbury, Wiltshire. The word "ank" (H-anks) comes from the Egyptian and means soul. Thomas Hanks III was a soldier under Cromwell and had four children. His son, Joseph, had five children, one of whom was named Benjamin. Benjamin Hanks and his wife

Bust of John F. Kennedy in London.

Woodrow Wilson's ancestral home in County Tyrone, Ireland.

Sulgrave Manor, the Washington ancestral home.

United States Embassy in London.

St. Martin's-in-the-Fields, London.

Westminster Abbey, London.

The library in Winston Churchill's home, Chartwell.

Abigail sailed to America in 1699 and landed in Plymouth, Massachusetts. Abraham Lincoln's mother, Nancy Hanks, was the great-granddaughter of the emigrant Benjamin and his wife.

The Hanks were an inventive family, and it is said that the first bells ever produced in America were cast on their farm on Hanks Hill. They are said to have erected the first clock tower in America, to have built the first silk mills run by water power, and to have made the first cannon. They were a talented family, with many doctors, lawyers, ministers, and writers among them. Louis Hanks, who died in England in the late 1920's, was one of the first interior decorators. In the family history which he wrote, he tells the story of an Aunt Caroline who married the tutor of the Comte de Paris and became involved in the siege of Paris during the Franco-Prussian War but survived because their Hanks relatives in England managed to furnish them with provisions. There are still members of the Hanks family living in England.

There are a number of Lincoln memorials in London, the best known being the bronze statue of him in Parliament Square, a fine replica of the one by Saint Gaudens in Chicago, presented by the

Lincoln monument in the Old Calton Burying Ground.

Statue of Lincoln in Parliament Square, London.

American people in 1920. In the large central court of the Royal Exchange there is a striking bust of Lincoln, carved from Indiana limestone by the American sculptor Andrew O'Connor. At the junction of Lambeth Road and Kennington Road there stood Christ Church, built in 1876. The spire of this church, ringed with stars and stripes, was erected mainly with American contributions as a memorial to Lincoln. It was the only part of the church that survived the war bombing, but a new church has been incorporated in a large office block. There are also memorials to Lincoln in the Greek Church on Moscow Road and in the church at Hingham, Norwich.

Theodore Roosevelt's mother, Martha Bullock, was a descendant of the Bullocks who emigrated from County Antrim, Northern Ireland. Roosevelt himself was married in the fashionable St. George's Church to his second wife, Edith Kermit Carow, on December 2, 1886. He was thus the second American president to be married in London, the first being John Quincy Adams.

During the late 16th century, London had had a large increase in population and prosperity, and Parliament passed an act in May, 1711, providing for the building of fifty new churches. St. George's was one of the fifty, and the first stone was laid on June 20, 1721, by General William Stewart, who had given the plot of ground on which the church was built. John James, one of Christopher Wren's assistants, had been chosen as architect. Although the site for the church was not large, James succeeded in erecting a building of great beauty and dignity. He even started a new architectural trend with the imposing, six-columned portico at the main entrance.

On March 23, 1725, the new edifice was consecrated by Edmund Gibson, Bishop of London. The new parish covered an area stretching from Regent Street westward to the Serpentine, and southward from Oxford Street to include the whole of what is now Mayfair, Belgravia, and Pimlico.

The east windows of St. George's are filled with beautiful Flemish glass dating from the year 1525. The organ was built by Gerard Smith, nephew and successor of Bernard Schmidt, who built the organ of St. Paul's Cathedral. Many distinguished organists have played in St. George's. Handel was a frequent visitor and he chose the first two organists for the church. Many additions and repairs have

Bust of Lincoln in Hingham, Norwich.

been necessary in the course of the church's 250-year history. The entire interior was given a face-lift in 1972.

St. George's Church soon became one of the most fashionable churches in London and has been the scene of many famous weddings, in addition to that of an American president, Theodore Roosevelt. It was here that George Meredith, the Victorian novelist, married Mary Nicholls, the widowed daughter of Thomas Love Peacock. Percy Bysshe Shelley and Harriet Westbrook were remarried here in 1814, in confirmation of their Scottish marriage in 1811. Benjamin Disraeli, Prime Minister during Queen Victoria's reign, married Mrs. Wyndham Lewis in this church in 1839. J.W. Cross, a New York banker, married Mary Ann Evans (better known as George Eliot, author of *Mill on the Floss*) in 1880, but tragically she died the same year. It was in this church that Emma Hart married Sir William Hamilton, in 1791. Later, as Lady Hamilton, she became the great friend of Admiral Nelson. During a period of convalescence after the loss of his arm at the Battle of Tenerife, the Nelsons lived nearby in New Bond Street and often attended services at St. George's Church.

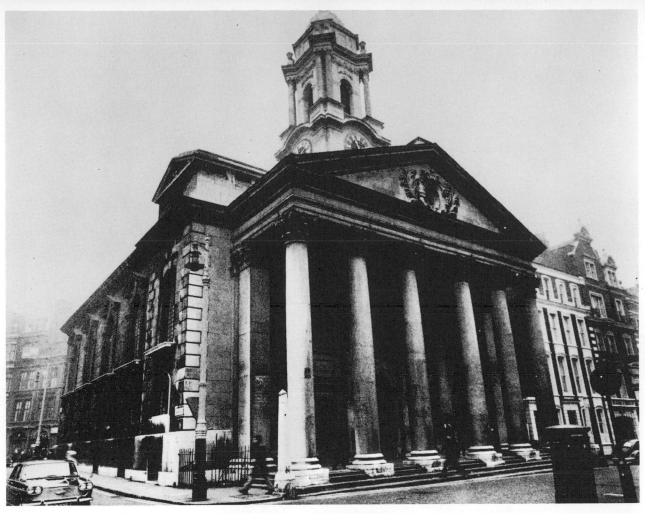

St. George's Church in Hanover Square, London.

The altar in St. George's Church in Hanover Square, London.

Interior of St. George's Church in Hanover Square, London.

Statue of Franklin D. Roosevelt, in Grosvenor Square, London.

The American Embassy, facing Grosvenor Square, London.

General Eisenhower's wartime headquarters in London.

Although he was married in the United States, Franklin Delano Roosevelt honeymooned in London, staying at Brown's Hotel after his marriage in 1905 to a distant cousin, Anna Eleanor Roosevelt.

A short distance from St. George's Church is Grosvenor Square, which has long been associated with the United States ever since John Adams, first minister to Britain (1785-88) lived at No. 9, in the northeast corner of the square. On the north side of the gardens of Grosvenor Square there is a large statue of Franklin D. Roosevelt, made by Sir W. Reid Dick.

The American Embassy, which occupies one complete side of Grosvenor Square, is a large, striking building designed by Eero Saarinen, an American of Finnish extraction. The American eagle, with a wing span of thirty-five feet, which surmounts the building, caused considerable comment when it was first put up, but people seem to have grown used to it now.

Opposite the American Embassy is the slightly smaller Canadian Embassy.

From June to November, 1942, General Eisenhower had his headquarters in Norfolk House, No. 31, St. James's Square. This had been the town house of the Dukes of Norfolk from 1723 until 1938. The house was rebuilt in 1939, and from it the Allied commanders launched the invasions of North Africa and northwest Europe. Interestingly enough, the first house on this site was the birthplace of George III in 1738, the monarch from whom America won her independence. Later, General Eisenhower's headquarters were moved to the north side of Grosvenor Square, at No. 20. From this time on, the Square was laughingly called "Little America."

In the museum at the Public Record Office, on Chancery Lane, there are several documents relating to America. In Case XII, for example, there is the "Olive Branch" Petition to George III from Congress (1775) with the signatures of John Adams, Benjamin Franklin, and others. There is also a map made by George Washington and a letter of his to his "great and good friend," George III (1795).

12

The Astors and Hever Castle

By an interesting quirk of fate, one of England's most history-filled homes, Hever Castle, came into the possession of an American. It was purchased in 1903 by William Waldorf Astor, the great-grandson of John Jacob Astor, who had gone to America from his native Germany in 1784 and made a fortune in furs and a chain of trading stations. William Waldorf Astor was born in New York in 1848, studied law, and became a member of the New York state senate. After three years as an American Minister to Italy, Astor moved to England in 1890 and became a British citizen. In 1916, he was made the first Viscount of Hever Castle.

The oldest part of Hever Castle was built at the end of the thirteenth century and consisted of a fortified farmhouse and yard, surrounded by a moat and approached by a wooden drawbridge. Two centuries later, a Tudor dwelling house was incorporated inside the protective wall by the Bullen family, who bought Hever in 1461. Sir Thomas Bullen (as the name was spelled in those days) inherited Hever from his father in 1506, when his daughter Anne was five years old. Thus one of the most famous queens of England, Anne Boleyn, spent her childhood and youth in this castle. Here it was that Henry VIII courted her, while he was still married to Catherine of Aragon.

On one of the King's visits, Anne was too ill to see him and remained in her room. When Henry learned that both Anne and her father were suffering from the deadly epidemic of sweating sickness, he sent his own doctor to attend them.

On her recovery, Henry came again to Hever, riding out with an escort of cavalry, who heralded his approach by the winding of a horn on a nearby hill. Those were the days of Hever's glory, when its name was familiar to everyone, and the goings and comings of those who lived there were on every tongue.

Anne became Henry's mistress even before he married Catherine, possibly because she found Hever Castle a dull place to live and welcomed some excitement, which the King thus provided. When Anne became Lady-in-Waiting to Queen Catherine, she lived at court, where she and the King had ample opportunity to see each other.

In 1526, Cardinal Wolsey sought to have the King's marriage to Catherine of Aragon annulled, on the grounds that it was both immoral and illegal for a man to marry his brother's widow. Failing to secure the approval of Pope Clement VIII, Wolsey had to step aside and the King took matters into his own hands. He influenced the "Reformation Parliament" in 1529 to pass a series of acts which abolished papal authority in England and made the King himself the supreme head of the Church. Henry VIII was now free to marry Anne Boleyn, which he did in 1533. A few months later, Anne bore Henry a daughter (Elizabeth I) and thereby lost favor, for Henry wanted a son. Anyway, he was bored with her by now, and had his eyes on Jane Seymour. So in 1536, Anne Boleyn was beheaded, by an expert executioner brought over from France, who used a sword from Calais instead of an axe, as was customary in England.

After Anne's execution her father was shunned or forgotten by his neighbors, but he continued to live at Hever until his death in 1538. Thereupon, according to British law, Henry VIII acquired the castle from his dead wife's family, but made little use of it except to grant it in 1540 to Anne of Cleves, his recently divorced fourth wife. It remained in her possession for the next seventeen years. Thus this moated manor house is filled with romance and tragedy, and it was the background for a chapter both sad and great in the annals of Tudor England.

Not until 1903, when Hever was purchased by William Waldorf Astor, did the old castle emerge from its three-hundred-year obscurity. Astor restored the fabric of the castle and redecorated the interior, adding some magnificent panelling and carved screens. In order to enlarge the house without detracting from the architectural design of the castle itself, Mr. Astor and his architect conceived the idea of building a village of cottages in the Tudor style to provide guest rooms, servants quarters, and other necessary accommodations—all inter-connected by corridors and adjoining the castle by a covered bridge across the moat. Changing conditions, however, made it necessary to reduce the rambling house to manageable proportions, so in 1963, the "village" was converted into a dozen self-contained and separately occupied cottages and apartments.

Until the restoration in 1903, there was only a modest garden around the castle, and beyond it lay a rank marsh, orchards, hop fields, and meadows. Mr. Astor had all this changed and converted into a magnificent garden, with paved courts, rose gardens, and topiary hedges, including a maze and a unique set of chessmen cut out of yew trees. There is now a lake of thirty-five acres, through which the Eden River flows. Overlooking the lake is a huge loggia with a colonnaded piazza, and behind it there are Italian gardens with fountains, cascades, and grottoes which form a setting for numerous figures of statuary and sculpture, which Mr. Astor had collected while living in Rome.

Hever Castle has remained in the Astor family since 1903, and is open to the public on Wednesdays and Sundays from April 1 to October 1. Upon William Waldorf Astor's death in 1919, the castle went to his younger son, John Jacob Astor, who in 1956 was named Baron Astor of Hever. In 1962, however, he and his wife moved to France and their eldest son, Gavin Astor, became the owner of Hever.

During the years that William Waldorf Astor was buying and remodeling Hever Castle, his eldest son, Waldorf, was meeting and courting an American beauty, Nancy Langhorne. Nancy belonged to a prominent Virginia family whose three daughters were all famous beauties. The eldest, Irene, married Charles Dana Gibson and became the original

Hever Castle, ancestral home of the Astors.

"Gibson Girl." The second daughter, Nancy, married Robert Gould Shaw, but the marriage was a failure and they were divorced in 1903. Shortly after this, her father suggested that she go to England for a season of hunting, which she passionately loved. On this trip, she met Lord Revelstoke, a spectacular figure who was very popular in society. He wanted to marry her, but she considered him a snob.

When Nancy Langhorne went to England a second time, in December, 1905, she met Waldorf Astor on the ship. Each was immediately attracted to the other. Oddly enough, they had been born on the same day in 1879. Waldorf was English by circumstances and education, though he did not technically become British until he was twenty, when his father took out naturalization papers in 1899.

Matters progressed happily for the young couple, and on March 8, 1906, Nancy telegraphed her father that she was engaged to Waldorf Astor. They were married on May 3 in All Souls Church, Langham Place, London, a church built in 1822-24 by the famous architect, John Nash. Being a divorcee, Nancy had first to obtain permission from the Bishop of London in order to be married in this church. The groom's father, William Waldorf Astor, was not well enough to attend the ceremony, so the young couple called at Hever Castle

to see him, before proceeding to Switzerland for their honeymoon.

Though they were both essentially American, Nancy and Waldorf Astor had long been in love with England, its social life, its sports, and its customs. Shortly after their marriage, the Astors bought an 18th century London house at 4 St. James's Square. A few years later they built a country house at Sandwich, Kent, which they named Rest Harrow. For holidays, it was an ideal place to "get away from it all." In 1909, they bought their famous house in Plymouth, and this is where the political action started.

William Waldorf Astor was very generous with his son and daughter-in-law and for a wedding present gave them the Cliveden estate, which became their principal home and for many years the gathering place of a social and political group widely known as the Cliveden Set. Nancy Astor's beauty and her American brand of hospitality were magnets that drew the famous from all ranks.

Nancy Astor never liked a tame life, and she was determined that her husband should have a political career despite a physical condition that made him prone to periods of complete physical exhaustion from time to time. She wanted Waldorf to enter the House of Commons and aim at a statesman's career. Accordingly, in 1909, they bought a house at No. 3 Elliot Terrace, Plymouth, in order that Waldorf Astor might become a Conservative candidate for Parliament from that district. Their house, in the southern part of the town, on the Hoe, remained family property until Nancy's death. Nancy put on an American-style campaign for her husband, going from door to door and asking people to vote for him.

Although he did not win on his first try, in 1910 Waldorf Astor was successful and was quick to make his mark in Parliament. Nancy's position as a leading political hostess grew accordingly. Nancy's beauty, charm, and intuitive understanding made up for any lack of formal education. Besides helping in her husband's political life, Nancy Astor led a very active social life. She often gave dinners in their London house for fifty or sixty guests, and several balls during the season with five or six hundred. She became a great friend of Margot Asquith, wife of the Prime Minister. Besides their social and political activity, the Astors went to Virginia every year to visit Nancy's father and sisters.

Buildings adjoining Hever Castle.

When the New Year's honors were announced in January, 1916, William Waldorf Astor was made a baron, much to the surprise, and somewhat to the consternation, of the entire family. Americans just weren't used to this sort of thing. In 1917, Astor was made a viscount. At the senior Astor's death on October 18, 1919, his eldest son Waldorf automatically succeeded to the title and was thereby forced to give up his seat in the House of Commons and become a member of the House of Lords. Six days after her father-in-law's death, Nancy Astor was invited to take her husband's place and become the Conservative candidate for the House of Commons from the Sutton Division of Plymouth. On October 26, she accepted the invitation and after a whirl-wind campaign, American-born Nancy Astor became the first woman to take a seat in the House of Commons, the lower branch of the Mother of Parliaments. British women had been given the vote in February, 1918, and on November 21 of that same year they were legally considered eligible for Parliament. One woman, Countess Markievicz, was elected to Parliament that year but disqualified herself by refusing to take the oath of loyalty to the King.

In her campaign, Nancy Astor had two strong factors against her: she was a woman and she was the wife of a millionaire. To counteract these handicaps, she made full use of her charm, beauty, intelligence, and quick wit. Her ripostes to hecklers and those posing difficult questions became known as "Astorisms" and were widely quoted. Nancy Astor's sparkling American personality was something new to the ordinary Englishman and he liked it. She was elected on November 28, 1919, by a 5,000-vote lead over her nearest rival, receiving a total of 14,495 votes. The crowd, awaiting the news in Plymouth, burst into loud cheering for the forty-year-old woman candidate. In her speech to the crowd of her Plymouth supporters, Nancy said that her success was really a vote of confidence in her husband, who had held this seat in the House of Commons for nine years.

The Astors left for London the next day and were greeted at Paddington Station by a crowd of admirers, reporters, and photographers. Nancy's one regret was that her father had not lived long enough to know about her success; Chiswell Dabney Langhorne had died the previous February.

After one day's rest at Cliveden, the Astors were ready to face a stormy Parliament on December 1. Not everyone in British political circles was as joyous over the election as the cheering crowds in Plymouth and at Paddington. A woman in the House of Commons—and an American woman at that! What was the world coming to! Even that arch Conservative, Winston Churchill, whose own mother was an American, was not pleased at the result of the Plymouth election.

The intrepid Nancy must have been apprehensive when she faced the crowded House, whose visitors gallery was also packed, even though she was supported by the presence of her husband, her two sisters, and her three older children. At the appointed time, Nancy Astor was escorted by the Prime Minister, David Lloyd George, and a previous Conservative Prime Minister, Arthur James Balfour, to the table of the Clerk of the House, where she took her oath of office and signed the roll, thereby breaking all precedent in this august body and instituting a famous "first" for women's liberation.

Knowing the violent opposition of Churchill and others to her presence as a member of the House of Commons, Lady Astor had the good judgment to make haste slowly. For one thing, she avoided the members' smoking room and seldom used the dining room.

Yew trees cut like chess figures, in the garden of Hever Castle.

It was nearly three months' later, on February 24, 1920, that Nancy Astor made her maiden speech in the House of Commons, and then she spoke on an unpopular subject—the law restricting liquor sales to certain hours. Possibly she wanted England to follow the recent example of America and have complete prohibition, but the English were in no mood for such deprivation and she knew that she dared not advocate such a measure. Instead, she argued for state ownership, and hence state control, of the liquor industry. Any curtailment of their drinking privileges met with great opposition, so Nancy did not increase her popularity by advocating this measure. Nevertheless, her speech was widely praised by her fellow Conservatives in Parliament.

Lady Astor's second speech in the Commons took place on April 14, 1920, and was also well received. Again she spoke on a ticklish subject— grounds for divorce. She was firmly opposed to making divorce easy, convinced that this was not the way to make marriages more happy. This, too, was an able performance and enhanced Nancy Astor's reputation as a clear-thinking, level-headed woman, who could present her views with clarity, emphasis, and charm.

Nancy Astor had long been an advocate of "Women's Rights," as they were called in that day, and on every possible occasion she worked to bring more recognition and opportunities to women, believing that they should have equal opportunity with men and equal pay. She was frequently asked to speak outside Parliament and rarely refused.

In September, 1921, a second woman was elected to the House of Commons and was warmly welcomed by Nancy Astor. Throughout her career she was cordial and helpful to all women who became members of Parliament. By 1931, there were fifteen women members of the House of Commons. Today (1975) there are twenty-seven out of a total of 630, and one of them, Mrs. Margaret Thatcher, was elected by her fellow-members to head the Conservative party, the first woman ever to be so honored.

In 1922, the Astors decided to visit the United States, and from the moment they arrived in New York, on April 18, until their departure on May 23, it was a round of entertainment, interviews, and speaking engagements.

Through the years, Nancy Astor was elected time and again to the House of Commons, in fact, whenever there was an election. Her majority varied from one election to the next, but at least she always won. In 1923, she succeeded for the first time in getting her own private member's bill passed, and she was jubilant. By the terms of her bill, the age qualification for buying alcoholic beverages was raised from sixteen to eighteen.

Desiring to commemorate the fact that his wife was the first woman to take a seat in the House of Commons, Lord Astor commissioned the artist Charles Sims, R.A., to paint a portrait showing Lady Astor being introduced to Parliament by David Lloyd George and Arthur Balfour. He presented the painting to the House in 1919 and it was hung on the main staircase leading to the committee rooms lobby, but it aroused a storm of protest from both sides of the House. The members resented the portrait of any living politician hanging on the walls of Westminster Palace. After a few months the portrait was removed and hung in Bedford College, Regent's Park, London. Later it was sent on loan to the University of Virginia, at Charlottesville. Meantime, in 1925, a rule was enacted that no portrait, bust, or other representation of any living person or any person deceased less than ten years should be exhibited within the precincts of Parliament except under very exceptional circumstances.

When George Bernard Shaw invited the Astors to go with him on a tour of Russia, they happily accepted. As a Socialist, Shaw was welcomed with open arms, but the Conservative Astors were not so highly regarded. When Nancy Astor innocently asked Stalin why he had slaughtered so many Russians, it immediately put a damper on their reception by official Russia.

When World War II broke out, the Astors offered the use of Cliveden as a hospital, as they had done in the first war. This time they made the offer direct to the Canadian government, which gratefully accepted it. Instead of a hospital, however, the great house became an evacuation home for young children and their mothers. A hospital was built on the grounds, however, with 480 beds and a research center.

The Astors spent most of the war years in their home in Plymouth, which was subjected to severe air raids that destroyed most of the city. Lord Astor, who was mayor of Plymouth, requested that the city be registered as an evacuation area, and 10,000 children were removed to safer parts of England.

In 1944, when Lord and Lady Astor were both sixty-five years old, they decided, though with considerable reluctance, to retire from Parliament. This was particularly hard for a woman like Nancy Astor, whose mind was so active and whose constitution so full of vitality. The very thought of retirement was anathema to her, but she gave in to her husband's urging and his reasoned arguments. In December, 1944, the newspapers announced that Nancy Astor would not contest her seat in Parliament again. In spite of this decision, Nancy later asked Winston Churchill, who was then Prime Minister, if he would use his influence to make her a peer, in her own right, so that she could take her place in the House of Lords, but Churchill refused to do so.

When the wartime restrictions on travel were lifted, the Astors were eager to visit America, so they sailed for New York in January, 1946. As on previous visits, Nancy Astor was widely sought for interviews and speeches, while her husband was primarily interested in having a good rest, somewhere in the sun.

Upon their return to London, Lord Astor sold their home at 4 St. James's Square to the government and bought a house at 35 Hill Street. The hospital built at Cliveden had been made over to the Ministry of Health. The Astors spent their time now at Cliveden and at Rest Harrow, in Deal, on the coast. The days of big parties were over. Nancy missed them, but Waldorf was too weak physically to partake of much social life. They went to the United States again in 1947, but that was Waldorf's last trip.

In 1949, George Bernard Shaw presented a bust of Nancy Astor, made by Strobl, to the Palace of Westminster (Parliament) and it was placed in the official residence of the Speaker of the House.

Although she was now seventy-one, Nancy Astor was restless without the "job" she had performed so admirably for twenty-five years. She often visited the House of Commons, especially after her son William became a member. One year she even attended, as a visitor, the formal opening of Parliament after the summer recess, something that she had never done before. Parliament had become such a habit that she could scarcely keep away from the place.

After her husband's death on September 30, 1952, Nancy Astor was more restless than ever. She traveled widely in Africa, Europe, and America. In 1958, she sold the house at 35 Hill Street and took an apartment at 100 Eaton Square. She celebrated her eightieth birthday on May 19, 1959, greatly enjoying it. Lady Astor was especially pleased when the city of Plymouth gave her the Freedom of the City that summer. This was the last public honor that was paid to her during her lifetime.

Unfortunately, her memory was failing rapidly, though her body was still strong. On April 18, 1964, Nancy Astor suffered a stroke and died on May 2, just seventeen days before her eighty-fifth birthday. She was buried at Cliveden, with a Confederate flag draped over the vessel containing her ashes. A memorial service was held in Westminster Abbey on May 13, attended by a member of the royal family, the Prime Minister, his predecessor, the Speaker of the House of Commons, and a host of people of all ages and classes. The American Ambassador took part in the service.

The great mansion of Cliveden, four miles from Maidenhead, overlooks the Thames Valley and is open to the public on certain days in the summer. Lord Astor had presented it to the National Trust in 1942. The mansion standing today, however, was built in 1950-51, replacing the original, which was built in the 1660's by the second Duke of Buckingham. It is interesting to note that "Rule, Britannia," which many people consider a second national anthem, was first heard in public at a garden party at Cliveden. That happened two hundred years ago, when Cliveden was owned by Frederick, Prince of Wales.

Italian-style loggia and garden of Hever Castle.

13

Jennie Jerome and the Churchills

Three American women have played a notable part in English history, the most spectacular, of course, being Wallis Warfield Simpson, who married Edward VIII. Nancy Langhorne was another, for she married Waldorf Astor and became the first woman to become a member of Parliament. Jennie Jerome was the third and probably the most influential of the three, by virtue of her marriage to Lord Randolph Churchill and becoming the mother of Sir Winston Churchill. But let's start at the beginning.

Like Nancy Astor, Jennie Jerome came from a well-to-do, socialite American family. Her father, Leonard Jerome, was a cousin of James Roosevelt, father of Franklin Delano Roosevelt. After making a million on the stock market, the Jeromes went to Paris in 1858, when Jennie was four years old, and they stayed there for two years. Nine years later they returned to Paris, but this time Mrs. Jerome took up residence there with her two daughters, Clarita and Jennie, but without her husband.

Now in her teens, Jennie was mature enough to benefit from the many cultural advantages of Paris. She was presented to the Empress Eugenia, wife of Napoleon III, both of whom were very fond of Americans, and the Empress took quite a fancy to the sparkling young Jennie. When the Franco-Prussian War broke out, in 1870, Mrs. Jerome and her daughters fled to England, where Leonard Jerome soon joined them.

After the sparkle of Paris, England seemed dull. Before long, however, they were swept up in a social whirl, and life was filled with dinners and dances, picnics and parties. On August 12, 1873, Mrs. Jerome and her daughters were invited to a special party on board the guardship "Ariadne," at Cowes, to meet the Prince and Princess of Wales and the Grand Duke and Duchess of Russia. It was at this party that Jennie Jerome met Lord Randolph Churchill, and they immediately fell violently in love with each other. Neither set of parents, however, was the least bit enthusiastic about the young people's plans to be married.

Randolph Churchill's father was the seventh Duke of Marlborough, and the British still looked upon American women, no matter how beautiful, charming, and wealthy, as being outside the pale, socially speaking. Queen Victoria, too, was said to frown on Anglo-American marriages, though she herself had married a German. The Jeromes felt that it was all too sudden, due no doubt to the impetuosity of youth.

Youth won out, however, and before long the young couple had overcome the prejudices on both sides. Jennie Jerome and Randolph Churchill were married in Paris on April 15, 1874. They took temporary quarters at 1 Curzon Street, London, until their four-story house at 48 Charles Street was ready for them. This house, very near Berkeley Square and in the heart of fashionable Mayfair, was a gift of Randolph's father.

When Randolph's brother married an American woman, Jennie went out of her way to introduce her to London society and to make her feel at ease in her adopted country. Anglo-American marriages were increasing in popularity—and acceptability.

As a matter of fact, there was now quite a rush among the titled and socially elite to form alliances with attractive American heiresses. One might say that Jennie Jerome had started a trend, and though it was slow in getting off the ground, it culminated in an American woman winning the top matrimonial prize of all Britain: the King himself, some sixty years later. When Jennie married Randolph, however, British society regarded such a marriage as "far out" as marrying someone from outer space.

The Churchills were visiting at Blenheim Palace, home of Lord Randolph's parents, when Winston was born. It was November 30, 1874, seven and one-half months after the wedding, and Jennie was no doubt taken by surprise. It was by chance, rather than design, that their illustrious first son was born in the palace. The birth took place in a small, rather austere bedroom west of the Great Hall, in the suite of apartments once allotted to the Marlborough domestic chaplain, Dean Jones.

Jennie Churchill may well have been a born flirt; at least there were always a number of men, including the then Prince of Wales, who were greatly attracted to her. Sometimes their attentions caused minor scandals, but nothing disrupted the Churchill marriage. There were also those who said that she neglected her children, turning them over to a nanny to look after. The boys' devotion to their mother throughout her life, however, would seem to disprove that idea. It was actually Randolph who gave little time or attention to his two sons, and the boys often felt very much neglected by their father.

Jennie was bubbling over with the joy of life, and it found an outlet in many forms. She was a tremendous help to her husband in his political career, campaigning with him and helping to write his speeches. Since 1874, Randolph Churchill had held a seat in Parliament as a Conservative. With this newly aroused interest in politics, Jennie Churchill became more and more attracted to intellectual activities, rather than the purely social.

A serious accident while playing a game of chase with his brother and cousin may well have changed the course of Winston Churchill's life. After the accident he was unconscious for three days and kept home from school for two months. The family had recently moved to the home of Lord Randolph's mother, at 50 Grosvenor Square, London (W 1). Winston was brought here after his accident and his mother devoted herself to keeping him occupied and happy during his two months' convalescence. Among other things, she aroused his interest in politics by giving him detailed accounts of what she herself heard and observed. She encouraged him to discuss political subjects, and she invited the outstanding statesmen of the day, including three future prime ministers, to their home for dinner. Jennie encouraged the boy to take part in the discussions and to express his own views, even when they differed from those of their guests. No therapy could have been better.

Winston's adolescent years, however, were difficult for the boy as well as his parents. For one thing, he had considerable difficulty in passing the entrance examinations for Sandhurst, the elite military prep school, and it was only on his third try that he made the grade. This was in 1893, when he was almost nineteen. When he received good grades and was given an infantry cadetship, his father was tremendously pleased. Nothing could have brought the boy into greater favor with his father. But the paternal interest came too late. On January 24, 1895, Randolph Churchill died, at the age of forty-five. As he had done throughout his twenty years, Winston Churchill would now have to depend on his mother for understanding and encouragement. For the rest of her life, Jennie gave it unstintingly.

In 1908, Winston Churchill married Miss Clementine Hozier in St. Margaret's Church, the parish church of the House of Commons since 1614. Other famous weddings in St. Margaret's were those of Samuel Pepys, in 1655, and John Milton, in 1656.

Now that she was a widow, Jennie had more admirers than ever, and her social calendar was always full. One of her devoted beaux was Bourke Cockran, a brilliant American who spent considerable time in England. Young Winston admired Cockran tremendously, and in later years said that this man had taught him the use of language as well as the most effective use of his own vocal powers. Though very much attracted to each other, Jennie and Cockran never married, but as a close family friend, he provided a father image for the two Churchill boys at a time when they greatly needed it.

In order to make a real home for herself and the boys, Jennie Churchill moved from fashionable Mayfair to a handsome Georgian house at 35A

St. Margaret's Church, London, where Winston Churchill was married.

Great Cumberland Place, only a short distance from Marble Arch and Hyde Park. When her two sisters moved nearby, it gave her a sense of "home," which had been sadly lacking since Randolph died.

Although Jennie Churchill had long been attracting men much younger than herself, English society was nevertheless aghast when it learned that she planned to marry George Cornwallis-West, a tall handsome man just two weeks older than her own son Winston. Both Winston and the Cornwallis-West family did everything possible to prevent it, but to no purpose. The forty-six-year-old widow and the twenty-five-year-old young soldier were married at St. Paul's Church, Knightsbridge, London, on July 28, 1900, in a ceremony attended by the top echelon of British society. The marriage lasted for twelve tempestuous years, ending in divorce in 1913, after George had walked out on her in December of 1912.

Jennie had been making history in her own way after the death of Lord Randolph Churchill. She founded the *Anglo-Saxon Review,* and greatly enjoyed her professional and social contacts with the prominent literary figures of the day. When the Boer War broke out in South Africa, she organized an American hospital ship to look after the wounded British soldiers. She sailed with the *Maine* to Durban, South Africa, and spent several months in looking after the wounded. A year later, the very day on which the divorce decree became final, George Cornwallis-West married the well known actress, Mrs. Patrick Campbell.

Five years later, at the age of sixty-four, Jennie Churchill married another young man, Montagu Porch, who at forty-one was three years younger than Winston. Jennie Jerome Churchill died three years later, on June 29, 1921, as a result of complications which followed a severe fall.

With such an outstanding American mother, it is not surprising that Winston Churchill made a notable reputation in so many fields: military, journalistic, artistic, diplomatic, and governmental. As Prime Minister of Britain after World War II, Churchill met his greatest challenge. He later refused the peerage that is usually given to retired Prime Ministers and remained in the House of Commons until shortly before his death in January, 1965, at the age of ninety. He died in his London home, at 28 Hyde Park Gate, which he had bought in 1945. It was the 70th anniversary of the death of his father. Sir Winston was buried in the Churchill family plot, beside his American mother and his British father, in the quiet country churchyard at Bladon, near Blenheim Palace.

As one of the most outstanding men of the 20th century, the world has paid many honors to Winston Churchill. He was made an honorary citizen of the United States in 1963, a distinction shared only by the Marquis de Lafayette. An outstanding writer and public speaker, Churchill was awarded the Nobel Prize for Literature in 1953.

On December 1, 1969, Lady Spencer-Churchill ("my darling Clementine") unveiled a statue of her late husband in the Members' Lobby of the House of Commons. The Speaker of the House, Horace King, escorted Lady Spencer-Churchill to her seat in the Members' Lobby and delivered a short speech before the unveiling. The bronze statue by Oscar Nemon is seven and a half feet high and weighs slightly less than a ton. Sir Winston is depicted with his hands on his hips, his head jutting and his left foot forward, as if he were in a hurry to get something done. The statue stands to the left of the Churchill Arch, which was built at Sir Winston's suggestion in memory of those who "kept the bridge" during the dark days of the war. It is made up of the stones which were damaged when the Chamber of the House of Commons was bombed in 1941. On the other side of the arch is a statue of Lloyd George.

Another bronze statue of Churchill by Oscar Nemon stands in the Guildhall, which is the famed Hall of the Corporation of the City of London, rebuilt in the early 15th century. On the green at the top of the hill in Westerham, Kent, there is a third bronze of Churchill by Oscar Nemon. This statue shows him slumped back in a chair, with his chin thrust forward. Churchill is memorialized in Westminster Abbey by a green marble stone between the grave of the Unknown Warrior and the west door. This was unveiled by Queen Elizabeth II on September 19, 1965.

Churchill's birthplace, Blenheim Palace, is one of the most magnificent of English houses and the only one, besides those belonging to the royal family, that is called a palace. It was given by Queen Anne to the first Duke of Marlborough as a mark of the nation's gratitude for his victories over the French and his crushing defeat of Louis XIV. Located at Woodstock, a charming small town with 18th century houses that lies eight miles north of Oxford, this palace is truly a masterpiece in the classical style. It was created by the famous

Scroll giving Winston Churchill honorary U.S. citizenship.

Statue of Churchill in Westerham, Kent.

Chartwell, Churchill's home in Kent.

architect, Sir John Vanbrugh, between the years 1705 and 1722. The palace is rich in treasures of china, paintings, tapestries, portraits, and furniture. The gardens and park were originally designed by Vanbrugh but later construction was carried out by "Capability" Brown, who also created the famous Blenheim lake. Both the general design and the rich furnishings are reminiscent of Louis XIV's Versailles. The palace is open to the public on certain days throughout the spring and summer.

A more realistic idea of Churchill's life and character, however, may be obtained from visiting Chartwell, which was his home for more than forty years. It is located two miles south of Westerham, the most western town in Kent. When Churchill bought Chartwell in 1922, it was no doubt the magnificent view of the surrounding fields and woodlands that attracted him, rather than the gloomy house itself. There has been a house on this site since the Middle Ages, built near the "well of the Chart," the spring that now feeds the swimming pool and lake.

Although it has become a shrine for all English-speaking peoples, Chartwell has not lost its "lived-in" atmosphere. In the entrance hall, for example, the umbrella stand is full of walking sticks, and in the living-room there is a small card table set for bezique. On the second floor, there are bedrooms filled with memorabilia: medals, photographs, military uniforms, and so on.

The feature of special interest at Chartwell, however, is the garden, where Winston Churchill spent a great deal of time and energy. One of his favorite spots was near the fish pools, and beside his chair there is still the box for fish food. The Marlborough Pavilion on a corner of the main lawn is decorated with a bas-relief depicting the Battle of Blenheim, won by Sir Winston's ancestor, the Duke of Marlborough. The work was done in 1949 by Sir Winston's nephew, John Churchill, as a birthday present from Lady Churchill. Between the years 1925 and 1932, Sir Winston built a wall around what was formerly the kitchen garden, and here also is the cottage which he made for his younger daughters.

The wall, incidentally, is not a common garden-variety type, but is nearly eight feet high, built stepwise down the hill on all four sides of the kitchen garden. It is said to be a copy of the wall around Quebec House, which was General Wolfe's early home. In order to conciliate the unions, Churchill took out a card in 1928 as an adult apprentice in the Amalgamated Union of Building Trade Workers. Churchill found it very relaxing to walk in the garden with his dog or a pet sheep. Among the little group of cottages near the wall there is Churchill's studio, with many of his paintings and an unfinished canvas still on the easel.

Sir Winston's study is the only room in Chartwell containing the original features of the old house. He loved this room, and it was here that he did most of his writing. The room is essentially as he left it for the last time in October, 1964. Among the special items of interest is the working desk, which was a gift from his children in 1949, and the first Allied flag to be flown in a captured European capital during World War II.

Plaque regarding the wall built by Churchill at Chartwell.

Churchill's dispatch box.

On April 9, 1973, a special exhibition of photographs, documents, and other Churchill memorabilia was staged at the American Museum in Bath, to mark the tenth anniversary of Churchill's being granted honorary American citizenship.

An Archives Center for historical research into the papers of distinguished men of the Churchill era was formally opened at Churchill College, Cambridge, on July 26, 1973, by the American Ambassador, Mr. Walter H. Annenberg. The Center was built and endowed by, or in memory of, American ambassadors to Britain, as well as admirers of Winston Churchill. Among those attending the opening ceremony were Prince Philip, Baroness Spencer-Churchill, Sir Winston's widow, and Mr. Averill Harriman, veteran American diplomat, who is married to Mrs. Pamela Churchill, the first wife of Sir Winston's late son, Randolph.

Churchill College, Cambridge, was founded in 1960 as the British national memorial to Sir Winston, and has since established itself as a center for historical research. About 200 collections have been contributed to the college, including the papers of more than 120 political, military, and scientific leaders. One of the oldest collections is that of Lord Randolph Churchill, Sir Winston's father.

14
Writers and Artists

Once the colonies were settled and their independence won, the Anglo-American relationship took a new turn. Aspiring novelists, poets, and artists now turned toward England for the furtherance of their careers. The history, accomplishments, and beauty of the British Isles had long provided the background for those literary and artistic classics that formed the warp and woof of American education. What could be more natural than to visit the scene of these classics and mingle with their counterparts on the other side of the Atlantic. Despite the Revolutionary War and the resultant independence of the American colonies, culturally speaking the umbilical cord has never been cut. Beginning with Washington Irving, in 1805, writers and artists headed East.

In Great Britain they found the things that every aspiring creative person needs—the companionship of fellow craftsmen and the inspiration of a sympathetic environment, as well as such practical aids as subject matter and background for some of their best creative work. Let's take a look at the Americans who established a pattern of travel and study that is followed to this day.

James Fenimore Cooper, born in Burlington, New Jersey, in 1789, attained world fame as the American counterpart of Sir Walter Scott. Shortly after starting his literary career, when he had had only half a dozen novels published, Cooper and his wife and their five children went to Europe and spent seven years there, travelling widely and observing carefully. When in London, the Coopers lived at St. James's Place (SW 1). Upon his return

to America, Cooper wrote five European travel books and then reverted to writing novels, which achieved great popularity on both sides of the Atlantic.

John Singleton Copley was born in Boston in 1738 and, by the time he was twenty-five, had become a popular portrait painter, with a distinct style of uncompromising realism. In 1766 his painting, *The Boy with the Squirrel,* was exhibited in London and received high praise from Sir Joshua Reynolds and Benjamin West. Both artists urged Copley to visit Europe, but he remained in America until 1774, when the political and economic unrest forced him to leave.

Copley and his family settled in London and lived at 24 St. George Street (W1). In 1779, he was elected to full membership in the Royal Academy. His most ambitious historical painting, *The Death of Chatham,* hangs in the National Gallery, at Trafalgar Square. Another historical work, *The Death of Major Pierson,* hangs in the Tate Gallery in London. Copley painted the portraits of many visiting Americans, including John Quincy Adams, John Hancock, and Samuel Adams. John Singleton Copley died on September 9, 1815, and was buried at St. John's Church, Croydon, Surrey.

Ralph Waldo Emerson, the well known essayist, poet, and philosopher, was born in Boston in 1803. He first visited England in 1827, when he was only twenty-four years old, and stayed at Cheyne Row (SW 3) with Thomas Carlyle. Six years later he returned, in 1833, and lived for awhile at 63 Russell Square (WC 1). The American writer made a third visit to Britain when he was seventy years old, and lived at 16 Down Street (W 1). The year before, in 1872, his son had been a student at St. Thomas Hospital, in Lambeth (SE 1). Emerson's book, *English Traits,* is based on a lecture tour through Great Britain in 1847.

Though born in San Francisco in 1874, Robert Frost is usually thought of as a New England poet, since he spent most of his life in that area. In 1912, at the age of thirty-eight, Frost took his family to England, where they "lived under thatch." His first two books, *A Boy's Will* and *North of Boston* were published in England and brought fame to Frost in his forties. The Frosts lived in Ledington, Ledbury, Herefordshire for awhile in 1914. Frost won the Pulitzer prize four times, as well as many honorary degrees and literary prizes.

Although born in Albany, New York, in 1836, Francis Bret Harte is best known for his poems and stories of the gold rush days in California. He came to England after he was well known as a writer and lived at Lancaster Gate (W 2) for some time. Bret Harte continued his writing in England, doing much of it while staying as the guest of the Duchess of Albany, at Bestwood, Nottingham. He also wrote while a guest of the Marquis of Northampton at Castle Ashby, Northampton. After serving as U.S. Consul at Glasgow from 1880 to 1885, Bret Harte moved to Frimley, Bagshot, Surrey, and lived there until his death on May 5, 1902. He was buried in St. Peter's churchyard in Frimley, and lies beneath a polished granite stone. The museum at Camberley, Surrey, has many relics of this great American writer.

Nathaniel Hawthorne is another American writer who spent considerable time in England after he became established in his profession. Hawthorne was born in Salem, Massachusetts, in 1804, but his people had first settled there in 1630. Hawthorne's ancestors, who originally spelled the name "Hathorne" came from Wiltshire, England. One William Hathorne went with Winthrop in the *Arabella* to New England and settled in Dorchester, but later moved to Salem, where he was given a large grant of land. As a magistrate, he is said to have been responsible for punishing several offenders for witchcraft, and they may well have been the inspiration for some of Hawthorne's stories.

President Franklin Pierce, a college classmate of Hawthorne, sent him to Liverpool as U.S. Consul in 1853. Here he lived in a house on Duke Street and later in one called Rock Park, where he had as his guest Herman Melville, author of *Moby Dick.* When his term as consul was over, Hawthorne lived in various parts of England: first at 4 Pond Road, London (SE 3), where a plaque marks the house. Later he lived in Redcar and in Whitby, both in Yorkshire, and in Leamington, Warwickshire. Hawthorne wrote of his many visits to Albury, Guildford, Surrey, where he stayed with his friend Martin Tupper. He often spoke of the Staples Inn, London (WC 1) as "this truly delightful setting." There is a memorial to Hawthorne in Electra House, near the Savoy Hotel in London.

Oliver Wendell Holmes, born in Cambridge, Massachusetts, in 1809, gained distinction in two widely separate professions: medicine and literature. Holmes made two brief visits to England, but it was long enough to supply material for a book. His *Our Hundred Days in Europe* is a tribute to the hospitality that he received in England on his visit in 1886.

Washington Irving, born in New York City in 1783, later in life thanked God that he was "born on the banks of the Hudson." When he was twenty-one, his brothers treated him to two years of travel abroad, so from 1804 to 1806 he made an extended tour of France, Italy, Holland, and England. While in England in 1805, he stayed at the New England Coffee House, on Threadneedle Street, London (EC 2). He returned home with manuscript notes and journals that were of tremendous value in his writing.

In 1815, Irving again sailed for Europe, this time to remain seventeen years. He spent a few days at Abbotsford with Sir Walter Scott, a meeting which moved him deeply. Soon he began sending to America installments of *The Sketch Book,* which included his best known stories, such as "Rip Van Winkle" and "The Legend of Sleepy Hollow." When his work was praised by the leading British men of letters, Washington Irving became famous overnight, and he soon became friends with the leading English writers of the day.

After an exciting winter at the court of Frederick Augustus in Saxony (1823), playwriting in Paris with Thomas Paine (1824), and three productive years in Spain (1826-1829), Irving returned to London to serve as American attaché for three years (1829-1832). He worked at the United States ministry in Chandos Street, in the days before it was an Embassy. His favorite haunt was the Boar's

Head Tavern, in Eastcheap (EC 3). During this period in London he lived at 35 Norfolk Street. Irving was fond of eating at Jack Straw's Castle, on Hampstead Heath (NW 3). This old inn, well known to Dickens and Thackeray, was commemorated by Irving in *Tales of a Traveler.*

When visiting Stratford-on-Avon, Irving stayed at the Red Horse Inn on the market place and wrote about it as follows: "To a homeless man, who has no spot in this wide world which he can truly call his own, there is a feeling of something like independence and territoral consequence when, after a weary day's travel, he kicks off his boots, thrusts his feet into his slippers, and stretches himself before an inn fire. Let the world go as it may, let kingdoms rise or fall, so long as he has the wherewithal to pay his bill he is, for the time being, the very monarch of all he surveys. The armchair is his throne, the poker his sceptre, and the inn parlour some twelve feet square, his undisputed empire." Irving's armchair and poker were for a long time lovingly preserved in this old inn.

Irving was fascinated by the Maypole ceremonies in Chester, Cheshire. In Buxton, Derbyshire, Irving remarked upon the eccentricities of the English people, while Aston Hall in Aston, Birmingham, Warwickshire, appears in his novel, *Bracebridge Hall.*

Upon his return to America in 1832, after seventeen years abroad, Washington Irving was feted at a public dinner and toasts were drunk to America's "first man of letters." He was urged, however, to transfer the locale of his stories from Europe to America, which he subsequently did.

Washington Irving's parents, both British, were married at Falmouth, England, in 1761. His father was an officer on a packet-ship running between Falmouth and New York. In 1763, the Irvings moved to New York.

Born in New York City in 1843, Henry James lived in England for most of his adult life. Interested in uniting European culture and American idealism, James aspired to write so that the reader would not know whether he was an American writing about England or an Englishman writing about America. First he lived on Half Moon Street, just off Piccadilly, then on Bolton Street, and later at 34 DeVere Gardens (W8).

The Red Horse Inn, in Stratford-on-Avon, where Washington Irving liked to stay.

Lamb House in Rye, Sussex, where Henry James lived for eighteen years.

For eighteen years (1896-1916) James deserted London and lived at Lamb House, in Rye, Sussex. This house in West Street, opposite the Church of St. Mary, is open to visitors one day a week. In his chapter on Rye in *English Houses,* Henry James wrote: "At favored seasons there appear within the precinct sundry slouch-hatted gentlemen who study her charms through a small telescope formed by their curved finger and thumb. Leading a train of English and American lady pupils, they distribute their disciples at selected points, where the Master going his rounds from hour to hour reminds you of nothing so much as a busy chef with many saucepans on the stove and periodically lifting their covers for a sniff and a stir. There are ancient doorsteps which are used for their convenience of view and where the fond proprietor going and coming has to pick his way among paraphernalia, or take flying leaps over industry and genius."

Henry James spent the last four years of his life in 21 Carlyle Mansions, on Cheyne Walk, Chelsea, between Cheyne Row and Lawrence Street. There is a tablet recording his residence there. When World War I broke out, it aroused in him such intense sympathy with England and her Allies that he decided to apply for British citizenship. On July 26, 1915, he became a British citizen and the following January he was awarded the Order of Merit. Unfortunately, the insignia had to be brought to him on his sickbed, by Viscount Bryce. James died on February 28, 1916. His epitaph in Chelsea Old Church reads as follows:

In memory of Henry James, Novelist
Born in New York, 1843. Died in Chelsea, 1916.
Lover and interpreter of the fine
amenities of brave decisions and generous
loyalties; resident of this parish, who
renounced a cherished citizenship to give his
allegiance to England in the first
year of the Great War.

Founded in the twelfth century, Chelsea Old Church is considered by many to be the most unspoiled old church in England. There is a bust of Henry James in the Chelsea Library in Manresa Road, just off King's Road.

Henry Wadsworth Longfellow was born in Portland, Maine, in 1807, the son of a prominent lawyer. In preparation for his post as professor of modern languages at Bowdoin College, Maine,

Carlyle Mansions, in Cheyne Walk, London, where Henry James spent the last four years of his life.

Longfellow spent three years studying in Europe, mostly in Germany, France, Italy, and Spain. He did spend some time in England, however, in Shalfleet, Yarmouth, Isle of Wight. Five years later, before taking a similar professorship at Harvard, he again prepared himself by study abroad.

Longfellow became famous for poems which cast a romantic glow over early aspects of American history, such as "Evangeline," "Hiawatha," "Paul Revere's Ride," "The Building of the Ship," and many others. His work was widely read in England and translated into many languages.

Longfellow's ancestors came from Guiseley, Yorkshire, eight miles from Leeds, and his grandfather emigrated to New England. There is a plaque in the Guiseley church that commemorates the Longfellow family. His mother was the daughter of Samuel Peleg Wadsworth, who counted among his ancestors the John Alden and Priscilla Mullens made famous in Longfellow's poem, "The Courtship of Miles Standish." Longfellow was the first American poet to be honored by a memorial in Westminster Abbey.

James Russell Lowell, who was born in Cambridge, Massachusetts, in 1819, became a lawyer before he took up teaching and writing. After he had made a fine reputation as professor of French and Spanish at Harvard (succeeding Longfellow) and as a critic and poet, he was appointed by President Rutherford B. Hayes as Minister to Spain and later to Great Britain. In London, Lowell scored a notable success, for he had the tastes of an English gentleman and was an effective interpreter of each country to the other. During his years in London, Lowell lived successively at the following addresses: 37 Lowndes St. (1880), 10 Lowndes Square (1881), 31 Lowndes Square (1882), 40 Clarges Street (1883), and 2 Radnor Place (1884). In his later years, Lowell returned to England in the summers, to visit friends there. He died in 1891 and there is a memorial to him in Westminster Abbey.

Walter Hines Page, who was born in 1855 in Cary, North Carolina, had an extensive and successful career as a journalist and editor before he was appointed Ambassador to Great Britain in 1913. Page was in close accord with President Woodrow Wilson prior to the outbreak of World War I, but during the period of American neutrality, his openly pro-British sentiments strained his relations

Statue of Thomas Paine in Thetford, Norfolk, where he was born.

with the President. The British considered him one of the best friends Britain had ever had in wartime. Page was married in St. James's Palace in 1915, while serving as Ambassador, and he had a home at 6 Grosvenor Square (W 1). There is a memorial to Page in Westminster Abbey and another in Pickering, Malton, Yorkshire.

Thomas Paine, whose brilliant pamphlet, *Common Sense,* was of the utmost importance in stirring the colonists to revolt, was born in the White Hart Inn in Thetford, Norfolk, England, on January 29, 1737. The son of a poor corset-maker, Paine had little formal schooling, and at thirteen became an apprentice in his father's trade. For many years he worked unsuccessfully at a variety of jobs in a variety of places and seemed destined to a life of obscurity and failure.

Paine lived on the High Street at Sandwich, Kent, and married his first wife in that city. They

119

Memorial plaque to Thomas Paine in Thetford, his birthplace.

Paine's last years were marked by ill health and the snubs of respectable people. Thomas Paine died almost an outcast. Ten years after his death in New York, William Cobbett, the writer and politician, brought the body to England, but no one knows where it is buried. A portrait of Paine, presented in 1916 by Mr. and Mrs. Curt Freshel of Boston, Massachusetts, hangs in the Guildhall of Thetford, Norfolk, his birthplace. A statue of Paine was also put up in recent years in the town of his birth.

Edgar Allan Poe, born in Boston in 1809, was taken into the Richmond, Virginia, home of John and Frances Allan when he was two years old, after the death of both parents. He lived in England with the Allans from 1815 to 1820, and went to school at 146 Sloan Street, London (SW 1). The family lived at 47 Southampton Row (WC 1). In 1815, they lived for a time at Irvine, Ayrshire, Scotland.

When young Poe was nine years old, he was sent to a private school conducted by the Rev. John Bransby, in Church Street, Stoke Newington. Poe describes the house, which is on the north side of the street (where Nos. 174-186 now stand), near the house that was once occupied by Isaac d'Israeli, Daniel Defoe, Thomas Day, John Howard, and many others less well known. The Allans and Poe returned to Richmond in 1820. Poe's ancestral family home is in Killeshandra, County Cavan, Ireland.

Though born in 1856 in Florence, Italy, of American parents, John Singer Sargent moved to London when he was twenty-eight years old and spent the rest of his life there, making many visits to the United States. Sargent received world-wide fame for his magnificent, lifelike portraits of prominent people of the day, and for his murals in the Boston Art Museum. During World War I, Sargent was commissioned by the British government to make pictures at the front. His London home at 31 Tite Street (SW 3) is marked by a plaque, and there is a memorial to Sargent in the crypt of St. Paul's Cathedral.

The famous American portrait painter, Gilbert Stuart, was born in Narragansett, Rhode Island, in 1755 and began painting portraits while still in his teens, though he had had no instruction in the art. His work was so good that it attracted the attention of a young Scottish artist, Cosmo Alexander, who took Stuart to Scotland for two years as a pupil. After a year back in his native

later moved to Margate, Kent, where his first wife died. In 1757, Paine lived near Long Acre (then Hanover Street) in London (WC 2) and later in Alford, Lincolnshire (1764-65). He married his second wife on March 26, 1771, in Lewes, Sussex, after living in the town at Bull House.

In 1774, Paine and his wife emigrated to Philadelphia and he threw himself into the controversy between England and the colonies. After joining the army and fighting in the New Jersey campaign, Paine was given a confiscated loyalist farm in New Rochelle, New York, and a small grant of money. For a number of years he lived here in semi-retirement, then went to France during the French Revolution and wrote his famous *Rights of Man.* The radicals under Robespierre threw him into jail as a harmless eccentric, and while in prison he completed his *Age of Reason.*

land, Gilbert Stuart returned to Britain and entered Benjamin West's studio in London. He stayed there four years as a pupil and assistant before he set up a studio of his own.

In 1792, at the age of thirty-seven, Stuart returned to the United States, living in New York and Philadelphia for awhile before finally settling in Boston. Stuart's fame rests largely on his many portraits of George Washington, which were widely copied and reproduced.

During the twenty years that he lived in London, Stuart had several homes: on Buckingham Street (WC 2), on Burlington Street (W 1), on Gracechurch Street, and at 14 Newman Street. For awhile, Stuart played the organ in St. Vedast's Church in Foster Lane, London (EC 2).

John Trumbull was born in Lebanon, Connecticut, in 1756 and took an active part in the Revolution, serving as aide-de-camp to General Washington. In 1777, he resigned from the Army in order to devote his time to painting. He was studying with Benjamin West in London, in 1780, when he was arrested and imprisoned on the charge of treason in connection with the hanging of Major John André. Edmund Burke and Charles James Fox secured his release and he went back to America. He returned to London in 1784, however, and again worked under Benjamin West. When Trumbull's paintings of *The Battle of Bunker Hill* and *The Death of General Montgomery* won great praise from French and other critics, Trumbull planned a series of paintings illustrating United States history. He returned to America in 1789 to arouse interest in this work, but went again to England in 1794 as secretary to John Jay. During his many years in London, Trumbull had several homes: at Adelphi Terrace (WC 2), at 23 Leicester Square, and on Welbeck Street (W 1) from 1799 to 1801.

Mark Twain, who was born as Samuel Clemens in Florida, Missouri, in 1835, grew up in Hannibal, Missouri. Like many writers of his time, he prepared for his career by becoming a printer's apprentice and setting type, as well as by wide reading and travelling. After he had become established as an author in America, Mark Twain visited England in 1872 and lived for some time at the Langham Hotel, now part of the BBC. On a later trip, in 1896-97, he lived at 23 Tedworth Square, London (SW 4). On a visit in 1899-1900, he stayed at 30 Wellington Court, London, while from July to October, 1900, he lived at Dollis Hill (NW 2). He also stayed at Brown's Hotel, as did many Americans of the late nineteenth and early twentieth century. Mark Twain was widely read in England and praised by many critics. Oxford University conferred on him an honorary degree.

Benjamin West, the famous historical painter, was born in Springfield, Pennsylvania, in 1738. From the age of seven, he was absorbed with painting, but his Quaker parents did not encourage this interest. Nevertheless, by the age of eighteen he was painting portraits in Philadelphia and then in New York. Seeing his talent, some New York merchants sent him to Italy to study in 1769 and he stayed there for three years. At the end of his studies he stopped off in England to visit, and liked it so well he remained there the rest of his life. Despite his humble background, West attracted the attention of George III and enjoyed the royal patronage for the next forty years.

West sketched or painted some four hundred pictures and brought about a minor revolution in historical painting by presenting his figures in the costumes of the period in which they lived. His home and studio became a mecca for American artists who came to England, and they all received great encouragement and help from Benjamin West.

On September 2, 1764, West married Elizabeth Shewell of Philadelphia, in St. Martin's-in-the-Fields, Trafalgar Square, London. Prior to his marriage, West lived on Bedford Street, London (WC 2). He had also lived on Castle Street, which vanished when Leicester Square was built, and at 14 Newman Street.

Benjamin West helped to found the Royal Academy and he followed Joshua Reynolds as its second president, in 1792. Many of his paintings hang in the National Portrait Gallery, Trafalgar Square, as well as in churches throughout England: at Sternfield, Suffolk; at Perlethorpe, Ollerton, Nottinghamshire; St. Stephen's Church, on Walbrook Street, London (EC 4); in St. Martin's Church in Ludgate Hill; and in St. Marylebone Parish Church, London. There is also a West painting, *The Shipwreck,* in the Greenwich Naval Hospital. West was buried in St. Paul's Cathedral on March 30, 1820, and there is a memorial to him in the crypt. His wife was buried in St. John's Wood.

James McNeill Whistler, born in Lowell, Massachusetts in 1834, moved to London in 1859 after four years study in Paris and lived there the rest of his life. When his painting, *At the Piano,* was exhibited at the Royal Academy in 1860, it was highly praised by the critics and Whistler soon became a member of the artistic circle headed by Dante Gabriel Rossetti. His dockland etchings and paintings of the River Thames, which show a poetic appreciation of the river atmosphere, won him great acclaim in the British capital.

Whistler became president of the Royal Society of British Artists but later resigned, with the remark that "the artists went out and the British remained." His work may be found in the Tate Gallery of London, the Glasgow Art Gallery, and in the Louvre, Paris. Whistler lived at 62 Sloane Street, London (SW 1) when he first came to England. Later he lived on Cheyne Walk (Nos. 101, 96, and 74) and on Tite Street (Nos. 35, 46, and 13). Whistler was living at 74 Cheyne Walk when he died, in 1903. He was buried in Chiswick Church.

It was when living at 96 Cheyne Walk that Whistler painted the famous portrait of his mother and also that of Carlyle. One Sunday, after escorting his mother to church, he painted a huge sailing ship on the two panels at the end of the hall. His mother was not pleased. She wanted him to put away his paint brushes on Sunday, just as he had to put away his toys as a child. At No. 101 Cheyne Walk he had a good view of the River Thames from his studio, a back room on the first floor. He could see the old Battersea Bridge and Battersea Church on the other side of the Thames. At night there were the twinkling lights of boats and barges and the glitter of Cremorne Gardens in the distance.

Bit by bit, English writers and artists began to discover that the United States had its own special charms, so the trans-Atlantic trek became a two-way operation. People of the theatre had long since found lucrative and prestigious opportunities in New York and Hollywood, but moving from place to place has always been a way of life with stage folk. Not so with writers and artists.

Edgar Wallace, the highly successful author of some 170 suspense novels, 300 or more short stories, and a score of plays, was eventually lured to Hollywood, where he wrote the scenario for the spectacular movie, "King Kong." Wallace died in Hollywood on February 25, 1932, but his body was brought to England for burial in Marlow, Buckinghamshire.

D.H. Lawrence, famous for *Lady Chatterley's Lover, Sons and Lovers,* and many other novels, came to New Mexico in search of a climate that would help him to combat tuberculosis. Two of his books, *The Plumed Serpent* and *Mornings in Mexico,* are based on his impressions of Mexico. After his death in 1930, his widow, Frieda, stayed on in Taos, New Mexico, where she became a legend in her own time.

P.G. Wodehouse became widely known as the inventor of Jeeves, the prototype of the proper English butler. During World War II, while being held in Berlin by the Nazis, Wodehouse made a series of humorous broadcasts to the United States, under contract to CBS. Although his comments were intended as satire, for a nation not yet in the war, the Nazis used his talks as propaganda and his fellow Englishmen regarded him as a traitor. Later there was a formal exoneration by the Foreign Secretary Anthony Eden in the House of Commons in 1944, but the issue was never quite forgotten. The upshot was that Wodehouse did not care to return to his native land and never did. Instead, he came to the United States and became an American citizen in 1956. He and Mrs. Wodehouse lived in New York City until 1951, when they moved to Ramsenburg, a village on Long Island. Despite his desertion of his native England, Wodehouse was honored on New Year's Day, 1975, when Queen Elizabeth II made him a Knight Commander of the Order of the British Empire. He died a few weeks later, on February 14, at the age of ninety-three. Wodehouse was one of this century's most popular, prolific, and durable writers of light fiction.

Alistair Cooke, recently best known for his book and TV series on "America," came to this country as a student in the early 1930's and decided to make it his home. Later he became an American citizen. His objective, clear-sighted observations on the growth of the United States have won him fame on both sides of the Atlantic.

15

American Philanthropists

Many American philanthropists have given generously to Britain, and there are a number of statues and memorials to show the appreciation of the British people.

George Peabody's name is probably better known to most British people than any of the others, because he provided homes for so many thousands of poor people. Peabody was born in South Danvers, Massachusetts, on February 18, 1795, and as a young man entered the wholesale dry-goods business. From 1815 to 1837, he was a partner in the firm of Riggs and Peabody, in Baltimore. After 1837, he lived in London, where he established a banking firm.

Peabody made a large fortune and spent most of it in benefactions to colleges and museums. He gave two and a half million dollars to the city of London to provide low-rental homes for workers. The apartment houses built with his money, known as the Peabody Estates, are found in many parts of London. Peabody was accorded the honorary freedom of the city of London on July 10, 1862.

A seated bronze figure of Peabody, with an appropriate inscription, was put up in the open space behind the Royal Exchange in London, at the corner of Cornhill and King William streets. It was unveiled on July 23, 1869, just a few months before his death.

Andrew Carnegie was born in Dunfermline, Fife, Scotland in 1835, but his father emigrated to America when young Andrew was only thirteen years old. The family settled in Allegheny, Pennsyl-vania, where many Scottish immigrants were then living. It was in the United States that Carnegie made his fortune as well as his reputation as a philanthropist.

The family was extremely poor, so young Andrew took a job in a cotton factory. He worked as a bobbin boy and earned $1.20 a week. His next job was as a messenger boy in the telegraph office in Pittsburgh, where he soon mastered the skill of deciphering messages by sound, rather than by machine transcriptions. He was then promoted to telegrapher, and was paid $6.00 a week. Eventually the superintendent of the Pittsburgh division of the Pennsylvania Railroad heard about this bright, ambitious lad and hired him in 1853 to be his personal telegrapher and secretary. When Scott was promoted, Carnegie was chosen to succeed him as superintendent. When Scott became Assistant Secretary of War, during the Civil War, he chose 26-year-old Andrew Carnegie for the important job of commanding and coordinating the military railroads and telegraph lines in the eastern U.S.

Carnegie had a shrewd business sense and after he persuaded the Pennsylvania Railroad to adopt the new sleeping cars produced by Woodruff, he was given a 12½ per cent interest in the sleeping-car company. He invested in oil fields and in a company that produced iron bridges to replace the wooden bridges formerly used by railroads. On one trip to England to sell railroad bonds, Carnegie earned $150,000 in commissions. This put him well on the way to building up an immense fortune.

Statue of George Peabody behind the Royal Exchange, London.

Memorial to Thomas Hardy in Bockhampton, Dorset.

While in England, Carnegie became friendly with Sir Henry Bessemer, inventor of a new process for making steel. Carnegie was not the first, but the eleventh, person to introduce the Bessemer method in America, but he did it on a larger scale than anyone else had done. After 1873, he gave all his attention to the production of steel.

Carnegie had been wholly self-taught, through extensive reading all his life. At one point, he had thought of becoming a writer and editor, but the lure of business was too strong, so he kept on with steel-making, paying unheard-of large salaries in order to attract the best brains of the day. In 1901, the Carnegie Steel Company was sold to a syndicate, which eventually became the United States Steel Corporation. Carnegie's personal share of the sale was two hundred and fifty million dollars and he spent the rest of his life giving away his fortune.

Andrew Carnegie firmly believed that men who earn great fortunes should distribute their wealth through charities for the benefit of mankind. During his lifetime he gave away three hundred and fifty millions. In addition to the hundreds of libraries that he helped to establish in the United States and his many gifts to colleges and other institutions, Carnegie provided hundreds of scholarships for British students.

Over a century ago, in 1866, Rodwell Wanamaker gave Westminster Abbey a great processional cross which has been used on all State occasions since then. On the Abbey's 900th anniversary, in 1966, John Wanamaker, a descendant of Rodwell, enriched that cross with twenty-two diamonds. The Wanamaker family is widely known for their religious work as well as for their large department stores in Philadelphia and New York City.

Stratford-on-Avon was presented with a beautiful Memorial Fountain on Meek Street, quite near Shakespeare's birthplace on Henley Street. Given by George W. Childs of Philadelphia, the fountain was dedicated to public use by Sir Henry Irving in 1887. Childs himself was honored with a memorial window in Westminster Abbey for his generous benefactions to Britain.

Another American gift in the same town is the beautiful window in the south transept of Shakespeare's church, unveiled by the American Ambassador, H.T.F. Bayard, on the poet's birthday, in 1896.

In 1882, American citizens placed a memorial

window to Sir Walter Raleigh in St. Margaret's Church, next to Westminster Abbey.

In the city of Peterborough, seventy-five miles north of London, there is a magnificent Norman cathedral. Originally a Benedictine Abbey stood on this site, founded in 655, but it was destroyed by the Danes in 870. A Saxon church was erected here in the 10th century, which was destroyed by fire in 1116. The following year the present cathedral was founded, and most of it was completed in the 13th century. Henry VIII's first queen, Catherine of Aragon, was buried here in 1536. A few years ago, a memorial to her was presented to the cathedral, paid for by subscriptions from the "Catherines" in America and Britain.

Americans erected a memorial to the famous English writer, Thomas Hardy, at Bockhampton, Dorchester, Dorset. Dorset is often called "Hardy Country" because it was the setting of many of the author's most popular novels.

A passage beside No. 3 St. James's Street, London (SW 1) opens to the charming little court of Pickering Place. Here the people of Texas have erected a memorial to Byron, who once lived on Pickering Place.

The great British poet, William Wordsworth, lived at Dove Cottage, in Grasmere, Westmorland, from 1799 to 1808, and later the house was occupied by the De Quinceys. It is now open to the public on weekdays. In the neighboring village of Ambleside, there is a memorial window to Wordsworth in St. Mary's Church that is in part a gift from American admirers.

An unusual type of memorial is that appearing on Christ Church on the Westminster Bridge Road, London (SE 1). A united Congregational and Baptish church, it was built in 1876 and the spire was a memorial to Abraham Lincoln, erected mainly with American contributions. The Stars and Stripes were incorporated in the design of the spire, which was the only part of the church that survived the war bombings.

Walter H. Annenberg, the popular United States Ambassador to Great Britain from 1969 to October, 1974, made many generous contributions to various charitable, educational, and religious institutions in that country.

16

Westminster Abbey

Probably the most revered building in Great Britain is Westminster Abbey, in the heart of London. Although by actual count, more people visit the Tower of London than any other attraction in the British capital, that still does not detract from the pre-eminence of the Abbey, which holds a unique place in the affection of the entire English-speaking world. Westminster won this pre-eminence partly because of the quality of its architecture, partly because it is a very large church ministering to the people of a very large city, and partly because of its age-old connection with the government of Britain.

Exactly when the first church was built on the site of Westminster Abbey is a matter of conjecture. The name occurs in a tenth century document in which it is described as an "awesome" place. Evidence seems to indicate that a previous monastery, or at least a church, stood on this spot, and legend attributes it to Sebert, King of the East Saxons, who died in 616. In any case, the supposed tomb of King Sebert, the traditional founder of the Abbey, may be seen in Westminster.

The recorded history of Westminster Abbey begins in the days of Edward the Confessor. Edward, who reigned from 1042 to 1066, was a prince of extreme piety, caring little for state affairs but worshipped as a saint by his people. Driven from his kingdom by the Danes, after his father's death, Edward vowed to make a pilgrimage to St. Peter's grave in Rome if he returned in safety to England. Once on the throne, however, he found it impossible to leave his subjects, and the

Pope released him from his vow on the condition that he should found or restore a monastery to St. Peter. This led to the building of a new church to replace the Saxon church of the Benedictine monastery. Hence the official name of Westminster Abbey is the Collegiate Church of St. Peter.

On an island in the River Thames, once known as Thorney Island and first used by the Romans, Edward set about to build a great monastery to promote the glory of God and the prosperity of his kingdom. Intentionally or not, he separated the seat of government from the City of London (the business and banking center), which lay two miles away across the fields. Hence the name "Westminster," or "west monastery," from its position in relation to the City. The King took up his own residence nearby the monastery, so that he might watch the progress of the building. By placing the Abbey and the royal residence side by side, he strengthened for some centuries the bond between church and state.

The consecration had been planned for Christmas Day, 1065, but the King was so ill that it was postponed, then hurried on and solemnized on Holy Innocents Day, December 28. By that time the royal founder was dying and unable to attend. On January 5, 1066, King Edward died.

After the Battle of Hastings, in 1066, William the Conqueror journeyed to London and was crowned in the Abbey on Christmas Day, 1066, thereby setting a precedent that has been followed by English monarchs for nine hundred years and also launching the great Abbey on its historic course.

For five hundred years, from the 11th to the 16th century, the palace at Westminster was the reigning king's place of residence. During this period, eight of the kings and queens of England were buried in the Abbey, though previously the only royal burial there was that of Edward the Confessor.

In the middle of the thirteenth century, however, the Abbey underwent a revolutionary change. At Canterbury and Salisbury, in England, and at Chartres and Beauvais in France, a more glorious architecture had been springing up, and Henry III decided that his own Westminster Abbey could be made more magnificent. He decided to pull down the Abbey erected by Edward the Confessor and start from scratch. He was fortunate in finding in William de Rayne an architect of ability and genius, who brought from France a perfect blend of the new French cathedrals, adding certain English touches, such as marble piers, a ridge rib in the vault, and a cavernous gallery, which gave the building increased richness.

When Henry III decided to rebuild Westminster Abbey, he seems to have had three ideas in mind: (1) to promote the glory of God, for Whom only the best was appropriate, by having only what was precious and beautiful; (2) to provide a fitting place for a coronation; and (3) to provide a suitable burial place for himself and his successors, near the tomb of Edward the Confessor, around whose body so much national sentiment had gathered.

The King lived to see the consecration of the east end of the new Abbey, in 1269, and he himself was buried before the High Altar in what became known as St. Edward's chapel. Before his death in 1272, the Sanctuary, the Transepts, the Choir, and two bays west of the Choir Screen had been completed. Henry III had spared no expense, but when he died the treasury was empty and the work stopped for almost a century.

As time went on, a swarm of traditions and legends grew up around the name of Edward the Confessor, who was canonized by the Pope in 1163. To be buried near those saintly ashes was a privilege that kings might covet. It is not surprising that Henry III, who drained the resources of his kingdom to build the church, chose to be buried on the north side of the stately shrine to which he

Westminster Abbey, London.

had moved the body of the Confessor. Since that time, king after king has been buried in Westminster, as well as the consorts, children, relatives, ministers, and standard-bearers of successive sovereigns. The feeling gradually spread that burial in the Abbey was the highest honor that could be paid to England's great warriors, churchmen, statesmen, and poets, as well as her kings. No church is more intimately connected with English history than Westminster Abbey.

From the thirteenth century on, Norman kings, monks, clergy, and the English people vied with each other in honoring the name of Edward the Confessor. They looked back to the peaceful reign of the pious and gentle Confessor, the last king of the old English stock, as to a golden age. To be crowned by his graveside lent an additional sanctity to the rite of coronation, and thus from the Conqueror to the present day, every sovereign has received the crown beneath this roof, within a few yards of the dust of Edward the Confessor.

The traditions surrounding a coronation in Westminster Abbey have been held inviolate. The coronation chair had been constructed by order of Edward I to hold the Stone of Scone which he had brought to London from Scotland in 1296. Since Edward II, all English sovereigns except two have been crowned while seated in this chair, the most recent being the present Queen Elizabeth, who was crowned on June 2, 1953.

After the Reformation, when all the abbeys were dissolved under Henry VIII, Queen Elizabeth I reconstituted Westminster Abbey as a Collegiate church and religious services continued, though the form was changed. In the monastic days, only royal personages and high churchmen were buried in the Abbey, but in the reign of Elizabeth I and thereafter, the nobility began to acquire vaults, and several very large monuments were erected. In the 17th century, many English poets joined the nobility, and Spenser, Dryden, Tennyson, and many others have followed Chaucer into the Poets Corner. In the eighteenth century there came the burial of people of distinction in other spheres: Dr. Johnson, representing literature; Garrick, the actor; Camden, the historian; Tompion, the clock-maker. Later there were musicians, scientists, architects, and prime ministers. The present-day practice of cremation, plus lack of space, has made it necessary to memorialize famous persons by small flat slabs in the floor rather than by monuments. Recent Prime Ministers, authors, architects, and Deans have been thus honored. Four hundred persons are commemorated in this Abbey, by tombstones, busts, statues, plaques, windows, or some other suitable memorial.

Structurally, Westminster Abbey today is just as Henry III planned it, although most of the outside has been re-faced. Thanks to Henry's inspiration, there is carving and statuary in every part of the building. It is not surprising that Henry III has been called "the greatest builder and the greatest patron of the arts who has ever occupied the throne of England."

The main piers of the Abbey are of solid Purbeck marble, and the floor is paved with a lighter variety of the same marble, mostly from quarries near Reigate. The arches are taller and narrower than those of any other English cathedral.

Although the multiplicity of monuments has interfered somewhat with the architecture of Westminster by blocking up windows, partly obliterating the arcade that runs around the Abbey, it is still one of the greatest examples of Gothic architecture in the world and contains many fine works of art in the form of monuments, pictures, plate, and fabrics.

The Abbey is 513 feet long, including Henry VII's chapel, 75 feet wide across the nave and aisles, and 200 feet across the transepts. The nave, 102 feet high to the vault, is the loftiest Gothic nave in England. The western towers of the Abbey are 225 feet high. Westminster Abbey is not a parish church nor the seat of a bishop. It is what the British call "a royal peculiar," as is St. George's Chapel in Windsor Castle. The Abbey is under the jurisdiction of a Dean and Chapter who are subject only to the monarch, and neither the Archbishop of Canterbury nor the Bishop of London has any authority over its affairs.

A feeling of awe, as well as reverence, comes over one upon entering Westminster Abbey, hallowed by traditions which form the very warp and woof of English life. In this very building, which has stood for over seven hundred years, the king and queens of Britain have been crowned, married, and buried. At first glance the visitor is impressed by the striking beauty of the interior, which is largely due to the harmony of its proportions. The nave is divided from the aisles by arcades of acutely pointed arches. Besides being the setting for coronations, royal marriages, and burials, there is one part of the Abbey—the octagonal-shaped Chapter House—which was the meeting place of early Parliaments for several hundred years. Westminster Abbey might well be called the embodiment of the soul of England.

Only by knowing its background can the American visitor fully appreciate the real honor that was conferred on several of his fellow Americans when a memorial to these men was placed in this great Abbey.

Two American poets, Longfellow and Lowell, have memorials in Westminster Abbey. A bust of Henry Wadsworth Longfellow, by Brock, was placed in the Poets Corner in the South Transept of the Abbey in 1884 by English admirers. This beloved poet had become a household name in England as well as America.

James Russell Lowell was known to the English not only as an author and poet, but also as American Ambassador to the Court of St. James from 1880 to 1885. He is honored by a window, with a portrait head beneath it, on the right of the

Bust of Longfellow in the Poets Corner of Westminster Abbey.

entrance to the Chapter House. The plaque reads: "Placed here by his English friends."

Another American Ambassador to Britain, Walter Hines Page, is honored with a white marble tablet just below the memorial window to Lowell. Mr. Page, who served at the Court of St. James from 1913 to 1918, will always be remembered as the "friend of Britain in her sorest need," during World War I.

On the south side of the Abbey, above the Warriors' Chapel, there is a memorial window to George W. Childs in recognition of this American's generous benefactions to Britain.

Near the west entrance to the Abbey there is a roll of honor, and above the case there is a memorial plaque to Franklin Delano Roosevelt, which reads: "A faithful friend of freedom and of Britain, four times President of the United States. Erected by the Government of the United King-

dom." This plaque was unveiled by the Prime Minister, Mr. Attlee, and by Winston Churchill on November 12, 1948.

On the pillar near the grave of the Unknown Warrior there is placed the Congressional Medal of Honor, the highest honor that can be conferred by the United States. It was delivered into the keeping of the Dean of Westminster Abbey by General Pershing on October 17, 1921.

Another American benefactor, George Peabody, was buried in the Abbey for a few days, then afterwards reinterred in his native state, Massachusetts. This information is given on a memorial stone in the floor. Thus, there are six Americans who have been memorialized in England's most famous church, among the total of four hundred persons so honored. In other words, 1.5 per cent of the memorials in the Abbey are for persons born in the United States.

There are several other memorials in Westminster that will be of special interest to Americans because of their direct relation to our country. One of the most interesting is the monument to Major John André, who was Adjutant-General of the British forces in America during the Revolution. André was sent on a secret mission to General Arnold, but was captured within the American lines, in civilian clothes, and taken before General Washington. In spite of every effort to obtain his pardon, he was hanged as a spy on October 2, 1780, at the age of twenty-nine, and buried beneath the gallows on the banks of the Hudson. Forty years later his remains were brought from America, at the request of the Duke of York, and buried with complete funeral service near the present monument in the Abbey. The bas-relief, erected at the expense of George III, shows Washington receiving the petition, in which André vainly implored for a soldier's death, instead of that of a traitor, and he is seen on the way to his execution.

The grave of another British officer in the American Revolution is that of General John Burgoyne, who was Commander-in-Chief of the British forces. He was forced to surrender to General Gates early in the war and returned to England in disgrace. Although later restored to royal favor, Burgoyne never fought again, but spent the rest of his life in a house near the Abbey, surrounded by his books. In 1960 his gravestone was identified and the name and dates were cut

Memorial plaque to Franklin D. Roosevelt in Westminster Abbey.

year of his life. His grave in the Abbey is marked with a stone in the pavement.

General Richard Phillipps, who served as governor of Nova Scotia for twenty-nine years (1720-49), is buried in the North Transept of the Abbey.

General James Wolfe, who won fame in his capture of Quebec, the capital of French Canada, is buried at Greenwich, but there is a huge monument to him in the North Ambulatory of the Abbey. It was erected by the King and Parliament in 1772, at a cost of three thousand pounds (then equal to about twenty-five thousand dollars). Two tombs were moved to make a place for the monument, which is a fanciful representation of Wolfe's death.

Of interest to young people of many countries is the memorial to Lord Robert Baden-Powell, founder of the Boy Scout movement. A stone in the floor near the Deanery entrance and by the Screen of St. George's Chapel commemorates his fine work. Above it are placed the flags of the Boy Scouts and the Girl Guides. The stone was unveiled on St. George's Day, 1947. Lord Baden-Powell died in 1941 in Kenya and was buried at Nyeri, in that country.

Some of England's greatest men, such as Shakespeare, have memorials in the Abbey although they are buried elsewhere. This is true of Sir Winston Churchill, in whom Americans take great pride, because his mother was an American. Between the grave of the Unknown Warrior and the west door of the Abbey there is a green marble stone that memorializes this great leader and Prime Minister. It was unveiled by Queen Elizabeth on September 19, 1965.

The Abbey has many memorials to the British who took part in the wars in America or against the American colonies. What is considered one of the best pieces of sculpture in Westminster is a memorial to Lt. Colonel Roger Townshend. This valiant young man, aged twenty-eight, was killed when reconnoitering the French lines on the second expedition to Ticonderoga. The bas-relief, designed by Robert Adam and Luc-Francois Breton and carved by John Eckstein and T. Carter, represents the fort and shows a skirmish between the French and British.

On the south side of the nave there is a memorial to another victim of the Battle of Ticonderoga, in 1759. This one honors Viscount

upon it.

Canadians, too, have reason to be proud of several of their own people who have been honored at Westminster. Canadian-born Andrew Bonar Law became a member of Parliament and made a notable career as a Conservative in the House of Commons, serving as Prime Minister during the last

Howe, who was killed in the first expedition to Ticonderoga. Wolfe called him "the noblest Englishman that has appeared in my time, and the best soldier in the British army." This monument was put up by the Province of Massachusetts before its separation from the mother country.

Richard Hakluyt (1553-1616) has often been called "the father of modern geography." He was one of the promoters of the South Virginia Company and gained fame from his writings about the discovery and settlement of America. He was buried in the south transept of the abbey.

Cecil Rhodes, who helped to develop Africa and who founded the Rhodes Scholarships to promote closer Anglo-American ties, is buried in the south aisle of Henry VII's chapel.

The Abbey is full of the work of unknown craftsmen of the Middle Ages, and much of it is very striking. Centuries ago, the interior of the Abbey was a blaze of color, for walls and tombs were lavishly decorated. The Cloisters of the Abbey are an ever-present reminder that this magnificent, awe-inspiring church began nearly a thousand years ago as a Benedictine monastery.

17

Runnymede: Its Significance and Its Memorials

It was the fifteenth of June, in the year 1215. King John and his supporters were drawn up on one side and the hostile barons, backed by many well armed knights, were drawn up on the other. They had pitched their tents some little distance apart on the long reach of level grass land which stretched along the banks of the Thames. The scene lay in Surrey County, on the meadow of Runnymede, between Windsor and Staines, twenty miles southwest of London.

For a full generation, there had been increasing opposition to the ever growing power of the monarchy. When King John made even more stringent financial demands in order to carry on his war with France, the nobles of the great landed families banded together and decided to have a showdown with the King. Not only had the King become too financially demanding, but he acted in too arbitrary a fashion as regards individuals.

The barons knew what they wanted, for they had long discussed their grievances. With great care they drew up a list of the changes they wanted made and the concessions they demanded of the King. Some were basic and practical, others were trivial. Above all else, however, the charter sought to provide safeguards against the monarch's arbitrary treatment of the landholders and his power of oppressive taxation. Each of the sixty-three clauses limited the freedom of action of the King in some particular regard. The principles of the compact they drew up have endured for nearly eight centuries. Not only Britain, but America as well, has benefited from the contract sealed on that memorable day in June.

Clause 39 of the Great Charter, however, was the most important of all. This clause provided that no man could be punished except by due process of law and after a trial by a jury of his peers. This one clause of Magna Carta—trial by jury—became a cornerstone of the common man's freedom, not only in England but in many countries of the Commonwealth and also in America. The ideas in the Magna Carta were exported to America in the 17th century and played an important part in shaping the American Constitution. This one document, the Magna Carta, has long been considered the first great step toward the constitutional rights of all men.

Unable to write, King John could not sign his name, but he made his mark, and the official seal was placed on the document. Thus it became the law of England. A committee of twenty-five barons was set up to make sure the King did not infringe any of the terms of the charter. For the first time, the idea was accepted that the King himself was subject to the law.

In the two centuries after John's death in 1216, the Great Charter was confirmed forty times. By the confirmation of 1297, it became the earliest enactment in what later became known as the Statute Book. Apart from certain clauses that have since been repealed, Magna Carta is still valid law in Britain.

The original parchment sealed by King John at Runnymede has not survived, but four of the many official copies made immediately afterwards are still in existence. Two are in the British Museum and two are in their original repositories: Lincoln

Cathedral and Salisbury Cathedral. One of the four copies of this precious document has been loaned to the United States during the Bicentennial Year. Each is written on a single parchment sheet, varying slightly in size between some 14 inches by 17-20 inches. They conclude with a reference to witnesses but have no signature. Their validity came from the Royal Seal attached at the bottom, though in three cases the seal has now disappeared.

Speaking at the ceremonies held on June 15, 1965, the 750th anniversary, the Bishop of London said, "Magna Carta fired the imagination of subsequent generations as no other document in English history has ever done. It has stood for freedom against the arbitrary exercise of power. Today as the nation celebrates the 750th anniversary of this Great Charter, it is reaffirming its belief in the principles which are enshrined within it."

Of the twenty-five barons elected to act as guarantors for the enforcement of Magna Carta, only seventeen left descendants. Many hundreds of Americans have proven claim to descent from one or more of these barons, and genealogists consider such descent from the first great declaration of freedom to be the highest hereditary honor in the world.

Strangely enough, no memorial was erected to commemorate this great victory until the twentieth century. What is even more strange, the memorial was put up by the members of the American Bar Association. In seven hundred years, the British had not seen fit to mark the spot where one of their most precious rights was won.

The memorial stands on a slight grassy rise, a little way back from the meadow, and it is placed within a ring of old oak trees. The heart of the memorial is a great pillar of granite on which is inscribed, "To commemorate Magna Carta, symbol of freedom under law." Over the pillar there is a circular roof in the form of a star-spangled blue dome, with an eye of light at the center and supported by eight stone columns standing on a stone base. When viewed across the meadow from the road by the river, the memorial looks like a small temple standing amidst its oaks. There is a simple stone path leading up to it, with stone paving and seats around it.

This beautiful memorial was dedicated on July 28, 1957, in appropriate ceremonies attended by more than five thousand people, including leading members of the bar in England and the United

Magna Carta Memorial at Runnymede erected by the American Bar Association.

States. The dedication at Runnymede was held in connection with the 80th annual meeting of the American Bar Association, which was held that year in London.

Above Runnymede on Cooper's Hill, where there is a wide view over seven counties, there stands a memorial to the Commonwealth Air Forces. It commemorates by name the 20,455 airmen who were lost in World War II during operations from bases in the United Kingdom and Northwest Europe and who have no known grave. This memorial was opened by Queen Elizabeth II, on October 17, 1953, and consecrated by the Archbishop of Canterbury. Runnymede was considered an appropriate place for memorializing the men who died in such a war. In her address, the Queen said, "It is very fitting that those who rest in nameless graves should be remembered in this place. For it was in these fields of Runnymede seven centuries ago that our forefathers first planted a seed of liberty which helped to spread across the earth the conviction that man should be free and not enslaved."

A gate from the fields of Runnymede gives access to a pathway of irregular granite steps rising steeply through the woodland. This widens into shallow steps of shell-marked Portland stone, which lead the visitor to the memorial to John F. Kennedy. The memorial comprises three acres of meadow and woodland, opposite Magna Carta Island, on what was formerly Crown land.

The centerpiece of the Kennedy memorial is a seven-ton block of Portland stone, taken from the same Whitbed quarry that furnished the stone for St. Paul's Cathedral. It contains an inscription which reads as follows:

This acre of English ground was given to the United States of America by the people of Britain in memory of John F. Kennedy, born 29 May, 1917, President of the United States 1961-63. Died by an assassin's hand 22 November, 1963. "Let every nation know whether it wishes us well or ill that we shall pay any price, bear any burden, meet any hardship, support any friend, or oppose any foe in order to assure the survival and success of liberty." From the inaugural address of the President, January, 1961.

The great stone block was unveiled by the Queen on May 14, 1965, in the presence of Mrs. Jacqueline Kennedy and the president's two children and two brothers. The Queen formally handed over the deed of the land to Dean Rusk, then the United States Secretary of State, to be held in perpetuity by the U.S. in memory of President Kennedy. The cost of the memorial was borne by public subscription, following an appeal by the Lord Mayor of London.

There is another memorial to Kennedy consisting of scholarships enabling young men and women from Britain to spend an academic year at Harvard, Radcliffe, or Massachusetts Institute of Technology.

NEAR THIS SPOT ON THE 20TH NOVEMBER A.D. 1214. CARDINAL LANGTON & THE BARONS SWORE AT ST EDMUND'S ALTAR THAT THEY WOULD OBTAIN FROM KING JOHN THE RATIFICATION OF MAGNA CHARTA.

WHERE THE RUDE BUTTRESS TOTTERS TO ITS FALL,
AND IVY MANTLES O'ER THE CRUMBLING WALL;
WHERE E'EN THE SKILFUL EYE CAN SCARCELY TRACE
THE ONCE HIGH ALTAR'S LOWLY RESTING PLACE —
LET PATRIOTIC FANCY MUSE AWHILE
AMID THE RUINS OF THIS ANCIENT PILE,
SIX WEARY CENTURIES HAVE PAST AWAY;
PALACE AND ABBEY MOULDER IN DECAY —
COLD DEATH ENSHROUDS THE LEARNED & THE BRAVE —
LANGTON—FITZ WALTER — SLUMBER IN THE GRAVE,
BUT STILL WE READ IN DEATHLESS RECORDS, HOW
THE HIGH-SOULD PRIEST CONFIRM'D THE BARONS' VOW:
AND FREEDOM, UNFORGETFUL, STILL RECITES
THIS SECOND BIRTH-PLACE OF OUR NATIVE RIGHTS.

J.W. DONALDSON, SCRIPSIT.   J. MUSKETT, POSUIT, 1847.

Magna Carta plaque at Runnymede.

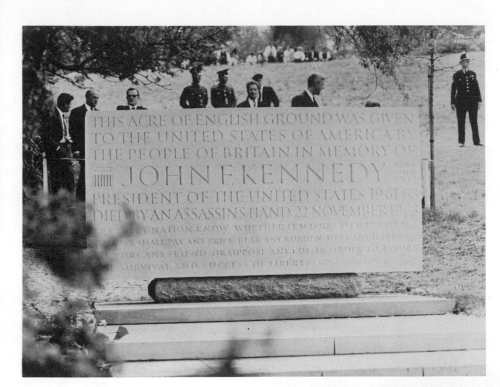

John F. Kennedy Memorial at Runnymede.

Queen Elizabeth and Mrs. Kennedy at the unveiling of the Kennedy Memorial at Runnymede in 1965.

18

The American Museum at Bath

Nowhere else in the world is there anything like the American Museum near Bath, and for that reason alone it is well worth a visit. It is housed in Claverton Manor, two and a half miles east of Bath, and can be reached via the beautiful Pulteney Street. Established in 1961, the Museum is open from two to five P.M., from March 31 to mid-October, except on Mondays.

The Museum was conceived by two Americans who had a deep appreciation of the American arts and a desire to increase Anglo-American understanding. Bath was chosen as a suitable locale for such a museum because of the old connection between America and the western area of Britain, whence came so many early settlers. It was also hoped that the Museum itself would prove an additional attraction for visitors to come to Bath. The Museum is now supported by friends in both countries.

Claverton Manor, where the Museum is housed, is situated high above the valley of the Avon River, with a magnificent view. The manor was designed in 1820 by Sir Jeffrey Wyattville, architect to George IV, and was originally built for John Vivian, an eminent lawyer from Cornwall.

The previous manor that stood on the site was a gabled Jacobean house, three stories high. It changed hands a number of times, one of the owners being Ralph Allen (1693-1764), the great developer of Bath. John Vivian decided to demolish this building in 1820 when the architect told him that the walls were not safe enough to permit of the repairs and additions desired by the owner. Therefore, Vivian erected an entirely new house.

By 1873, the present manor belonged to the Shrines of Warleigh, whose arms appear in the pediment on the south facade and over the front door. It was bought for the Museum in 1958, with some fifty-five acres of gardens, pastures, and woods.

Built of Bath stone, the south side of the house displays a classical facade combining a pediment with pilasters atop a rusticated basement. On the east side, there are two monumental projecting bays in the neo-classical style. These architectural features were common to late 18th and early 19th century design in both England and America.

Twenty furnished rooms, ranging in date from 1680 to the Civil War, form the nucleus of the Museum. The collections here are unique in Europe. American panelled rooms, with doorways, floors, beams, windows, fireplaces, and even a staircase, have been dismantled and, with their contents, shipped across the Atlantic where they have been reassembled piece by piece. For the first time anywhere outside the United States, the American decorative arts can be appraised in their original room settings.

The exhibits of earlier rooms show that the British settlers, in spite of dangers from disease, attacks from Indians, and a tremendous struggle for existence, managed to create homes of comfort and beauty, related in style, yet with their own individuality, to those they left behind in England.

The later rooms, beginning in 1775, give a

Claverton Manor, home of the American Museum.

glimpse of the more elegant life led by the well-to-do merchants in Baltimore, Philadelphia, and New York. Other rooms, such as the Pennsylvania Dutch and Shaker rooms, indicate the diversity of cultural and religious backgrounds that make up the American scene. In vivid contrast to them are the American Indian collection and the New Mexico rooms.

By the latter part of the 17th century, the settlers in New England had advanced considerably beyond the primitive cabins or simple wigwams of the early pioneers. They now had well built houses modeled on the English homes which they knew. On the first floor of the American Museum there is a low-ceilinged "keeping room," dominated by a huge fireplace, which served as a living-and-dining-room. It is constructed with beams and floor boards brought from a house in Wrentham, Massachusetts, that was built about 1690. The room is furnished with some original furniture from New England, including a pedestal table that once belonged to Peregrine White, born in 1620 aboard the *Mayflower* in Cape Cod Harbor. Another

combination living- and-dining-room, called the Lee Room, displays a table arranged for an afternoon meal, with bannister-back chairs.

Among the various rooms furnished in the style of the early 1700's is a "borning room," which was a small guest chamber conveniently located near the kitchen and often used in time of childbirth. It also served during illnesses and was sometimes called the "measles room." The child's bed could be easily "trundled" out from beneath the four-poster bed.

There is one room, called the Perley Parlor, taken from the home of Captain William Perley, who was a leader of the Minute Men and a commander during the Battle of Bunker Hill. At this period, many village homes had pine panneling grained to look like cedar, and pilasters painted to look like marble. The room also shows, in several side chairs, the curving line that was introduced in English furniture during Queen Anne's reign. The Connecticut highboy on display is the work of a rural cabinet maker. Although this style died out in England, it continued to be popular in America for some years.

Room in the American Museum whose furnishings all came from
a Massachusetts home.

The Deming Parlor contains woodwork and panelling taken from the home of Jonathan Deming, an officer in the Continental Army and a prosperous merchant. His home was built in 1788 in Colchester, Connecticut. The room also contains fine pieces of furniture by Connecticut and New York cabinet makers.

The Deer Park Parlor represents a typical 18th century parlor from Baltimore County, Maryland, and shows the changing tastes of the new republic. The influence of Hepplewhite and Sheraton, in which inlays and veneers replace the earlier carved surfaces, may be noticed here.

In a small bedroom from the Joshua La Salle house of Windham, Connecticut, there are painted and stencilled decorations on most of the furnishings and the walls.

In 18th century America, a flourishing economy encouraged a brisk furniture trade. Although inspired by English designs, cabinet-makers interpreted foreign styles in their own way and their works show the effect of different regional influences. The fashionable and prosperous city of Philadelphia became a leading American center for Chippendale-style furniture and some of the work produced in the colonial period has never been surpassed.

Besides the furnished rooms, there are also exhibits of glass, pewter, silver, needlework, hooked rugs, and a collection of American historical documents and maps. Although not required to mark their work, many craftsmen did identify their pieces, and the eagle was widely used in pewter designs after the Revolution. In the Textile Room there is a fine display of American quilts, the earliest dated 1777 and showing a Rising Star design. There are also hooked rugs, woven coverlets, and loomed homespun. The American "quilting bee" became a custom of the early days because of the great distances between houses and the lack of opportunities for social gatherings. Thus the "quilting bee," like the "barn raising" and "corn husking" offered a welcome opportunity for meeting neighbors and for combining work with visiting.

The Museum thus presents a three-dimensional picture of the historical development of the arts of the United States, the only comprehensive exhibition of Americana in Europe. It provides an opportunity to understand the American of the Colonial period and of the early Republic in a context of the rooms in which he lived and worked, the decorative and fine arts and crafts which he produced, and the gardens which he knew. Altogether, this Museum combines elements of the traditional art museum, the historic house museum, and the open-air village museum so popular in Scandinavia.

The park and formal gardens around the house provide an ideal setting for outdoor exhibits. The old stables have been adapted to make a gallery housing the Folk Art collection.

Two rooms of special interest are the New England Country Store and Postoffice, with its "stock" of more than a thousand items, and Conkey's Tavern-Kitchen, with its quarter-circle bar and open fireplace, where the Tavern cook can be seen baking gingerbread in a "beehive" oven, just as it was done 180 years ago.

The importance of the rivers, lakes, and ocean in the settling of America and in establishing her commerce has not been neglected in the displays in the American Museum. Life on the river is illustrated in scenes of the mighty Mississippi and of the Hudson, proving grounds for the first steamboat. Posters and early cartoons tell the story of the millions of immigrants to America. American naval history is shown in scenes of famous engagements in the War of 1812 and the Civil War. Reminders of the rigorous life of whaling men are found in the form of sailors' scrimshaw (carved and engraved whalebone) and harpoons.

The opening of the West is shown in showcases that display Colt and Remington pistols, a Wells Fargo strongbox used to carry gold, and many colored engravings that trace the development of transportation from the stagecoach and the Pony Express to the great transcontinental railroads. A variety of works by Indian craftsmen shows many facets of the domestic and ceremonial life of these first Americans. What was once the Spanish part of the United States is represented by a room built of adobe and containing the furniture of the period.

Visitors may have tea in the tea rooms or on the terrace, while enjoying the beautiful view across the valley. After "doing" the manor itself, they will want to see the Conestoga wagon, with original fittings and equipment, that stands near the tea rooms. This type of wagon was developed to meet the need for a strong vehicle which could negotiate the rough, mountainous area of the colonial frontier. It was first used for hauling produce and later carried supplies for the armies during the Revolution. In the 19th century, a modified version, which carried the settlers on their long journey westward, was called the Prairie Schooner.

In the 1890's, the Pullman Company built parlor cars which formed the last car on a train, and at the rear end there was an Observation Platform, so that passengers could get the best possible view of the country through which they were travelling. Presidential candidates often appeared on these platforms and spoke to the crowds in the towns through which the train passed. Singers and actresses often made a grand exit to waving admirers from these same platforms.

A reproduction of an Indian tepee as made by the northern Cheyenne Indians is of special interest to young visitors. The word "tepee" comes from the Sioux dialect and means dwelling. Not to be confused with the wigwam made of bark, the tepee was originally covered with buffalo hides. When these became scarce, the tepee was made of canvas or calico.

The early colonists made great use of the herbs which they brought with them from Europe, as well as other herbs which they obtained from the Indians. They used them not only for seasoning their food, but for medicine, as scent, and for making dyes. In the herb shop at the Museum there are bunches of pungent herbs hung up to dry, and spice jars line the shelves.

Taking gingerbread from the oven, in the American Museum.

Post office and general store, in the American Museum.

When George Washington was enlarging the garden of Mt. Vernon, in 1785, the Fairfaxes of Writhington, near Bath, sent him plants and seeds and even a farmer! Here in the grounds of the American Museum is a replica of his garden, bounded by a white picket fence. This garden is a gift from the Colonial Dames of America. Many of the displays and much of the furniture throughout the Museum were given by patriotically minded American citizens, who wanted the early history and way of life in the United States to be better known and understood by the people of Britain.

From eighty to a hundred thousand people visit the American Museum every year. Most of the visitors are British, and many of them are young people, who often come in school groups. The John Judkyn Memorial, which is handled by the trustees of the American Museum in Britain, makes short-term loans to schools and colleges of objects that relate to the history of the United States.

The city of Bath is one of the most fascinating and beautiful cities in England, not only for its Roman baths, its Abbey, its famed Pump Room, and its excellent Georgian architecture, but also because of the many associations with famous persons. It has attracted, as residents, an unusual

Conestoga Wagon, in the grounds of the American Museum

number of outstanding people in all fields of activity: statesmen, painters, writers, doctors, preachers, actors, architects, musicians, military men, historians, and scientists. Major John André lived at No. 22 The Circus, and General Wolfe, hero of Quebec, had a home at 5 Trim Street. Both places are marked with a plaque.

Indian tepee in the grounds of the American Museum.

19

Marriages and Memorials

Besides presidents and generals, statesmen and workers in the creative arts, many other Americans have received recognition in Britain. Some were British-born, others were born in the United States after it became an independent country.

Phillips Brooks, born in Boston in 1835, graduated with honors from Harvard and became rector of the Church of the Advent in Philadelphia. The prayer that he delivered at Harvard in 1865 at the same service in which James Russell Lowell gave his Commemoration Ode, won him national recognition. In 1869, Brooks was called to Trinity Church in Boston, where he remained as rector until he became the fifth Bishop of the Episcopal Church in Massachusetts, in 1891. He was a powerful orator and his fame as a preacher spread to England, which he frequently visited. There is a memorial window to Phillips Brooks in the south aisle of St. Margaret's Church, next to Westminster Abbey.

Born in Somersetshire, England, in 1566, Sir Ferdinando Gorges served as a soldier in the Low Countries, Portugal, and Normandy. In 1605, he undertook to provide a home and education for three American Indians brought back to Bristol. After they learned to speak English, they told him such fascinating things about their country that he sent several expeditions to America to found a colony there. In 1622, a grant of the land between the Merrimac and Kennebec rivers was given to him and John Mason. His early attempts at colonizing were not successful, but in 1639 he was granted a royal charter giving him governmental rights over the province of Maine. Although Gorges himself never went to America, he was considered the founder of Maine and the city of York, in Maine, was first called Gorgeanna in his honor.

Although Sir Ferdinando was baptized at Wraxall, in Somerset, where his family owned the manor house, there is a memorial to him in the Church of St. Budeaux, in Devon, a mile north of Plymouth. In this little church, built in 1563, where Sir Francis Drake was married and where his first wife was buried, are the tombs of Gorges' ancestors. The inscription states that the memorial to him was restored by the Historical Society and Citizens of Maine in memory of Sir Ferdinando Gorges. The memorial stands at the east end of the north aisle. There is also a church memorial to Gorges at Ashley, near Bath, Somerset.

Christopher Jones, master of the *Mayflower,* was married in St. Mary's Church, in Harwich, Essex, in 1593. That church was pulled down in 1819 and the present church was put up. The old tombstones were moved, as well as the 12th century font. At the west end of the church is a copy of Jones's marriage entry, while at No. 21 King Street, near its junction with the harbor front, is the house where he lived. A plaque over the door identifies the two-story house with an archway. Christopher Jones was buried in St. Mary's Church, in Rotherhithe Street, London (SE 16).

American Roll of Honor in St. Clement Dane's Church in the Strand, London.

General Richard Nicolls was born in Ampthill, Bedfordshire, in 1624. He commanded a troop of cavalry in the Royalist Army and in 1664 was sent to America to settle disputes among the New England colonies and also to take New Netherlands (New York) from the Dutch. Peter Stuyvesant surrendered New Amsterdam (New York City) to Nicolls on August 26, 1664. Nicolls changed the name of the province and its chief city to New York, and became the first governor. He was killed in a naval battle during the Anglo-Dutch War and was buried in the parish church of Ampthill, Bedfordshire. The cannon ball which ended his existence is embedded in the monument erected to him in that church.

Edward Winslow, a passenger on the *Mayflower,* was born in 1595 and baptized in St. Peter's Church, Droitwich, Worcestershire. Winslow was three times Governor of New Plymouth, and he came to London several times on behalf of the New Plymouth Colony. During World War II, a bronze tablet in Winslow's memory was unveiled in St. Peter's in the presence of members of the American diplomatic corps and many American soldiers stationed in the area. More recently, a reredos (screen behind the altar) was placed in St. Dunstan's Church in Fleet Street, London, often known as St. Dunstan-in-the-west. This octagonal church on the north side of Fleet Street has a 13th century foundation, but was rebuilt in 1829-33 by John Shaw and repaired in 1950. The clock of 1671 with its "striking jacks" was replaced in 1936. This church is said to have one of the most religious interiors in central London.

John Winthrop, born at Edwardstone, Suffolk, in 1588, studied law in London, but owing to financial difficulties and the problem of adjusting his Puritan conscience to the atmosphere of Cavalier England, he joined the newly chartered Massachusetts Bay Company in 1629. Elected governor of the company and of the colony, he went to Massachusetts in 1630 with some seven hundred colonists, who were soon joined by twelve hundred more. Winthrop settled first at Charlestown but soon moved to Boston. He was twelve times elected governor of the Massachusetts Colony and was founder and first president of the New England Confederation. In St. Bartholomew's Church in Groton, scarcely a mile from the village where Winthrop was born, there are brasses and memorials of his ancestors and two of his four wives. There are stained glass windows, given by Winthrop's American descendants, that commemorate John Winthrop and his son John, who

143

became Governor of Connecticut.

John Mason, born in King's Lynn (Lynn Regis), Norfolk, was appointed Governor of Newfoundland in 1615. With Sir Ferdinando Gorges, he obtained a large grant of land and went with a few settlers in 1623 to colonize it. Following this trip, he wrote a description of Newfoundland and completed a map of its coast. In 1629, he received another grant of land, which he named New Hampshire. Mason became vice-president of the Council for New England in 1632 and vice-admiral of New England in 1636, although he was a Royalist and not a Puritan. In 1691, Mason's rights in New Hampshire were bought by Samuel Allen. Because he had lived for a time in Portsmouth, New Hampshire, seven prominent citizens of that town placed a tablet to Mason in the Royal Garrison Church of Portsmouth, England. In the High Street of that same town is Buckingham House, where Mason once lived.

Although Reverend John White, born in 1575 in the village of Stanton St. John, near Oxford, never crossed the Atlantic, he is considered the founder of Dorchester, Massachusetts. He won this distinction because he gave so generously of his means to finance the colony that settled there. The house where White was born is still standing by the church, with a stone over the door. He was buried in St. Peter's in Dorchester, Dorset, where he was a Rector for many years. In the church there is a memorial plaque stating that "his name lives in unfading remembrance" in the Massachusetts Bay Colony.

Sir Richard Grenville, a cousin of Sir Walter Raleigh, was born in 1541. He commanded an expedition to North Carolina in 1585 and left the colonists on Roanoke Island. When Grenville returned the following year with supplies, he found that the colonists had gone back to England with Sir Francis Drake. He brought an American Indian back to England with him, but this transplanted redskin did not live a year. The house in which Grenville lived still stands in All Halland Street, Bideford, Devon. In St. Mary's Church, near by, there is a canopied tomb of one of Sir Richard's ancestors.

Captain Miles Standish, born in Duxbury, Lancaster, England, sailed with the Pilgrims on the *Mayflower* in 1620. During the colony's first five years, he was of invaluable assistance, in helping the sick, fortifying the colony, and establishing peaceful relations with the Indians. In the church of St. Lawrence, in Duxbury, there is a Standish Chapel, with memorials of the family. The present Duxbury Hall occupies the site of Miles Standish' birthplace. With John Alden, he founded Duxbury, Massachusetts, in 1631 and spent the rest of his life there.

In Billericay, Essex, there is a Mayflower Hall containing a memorial to four of the company that followed the Pilgrims to the New World: Solomon Prower, John Langerman, Marie and Christopher Martin. They had all lived in the neighborhood of Billericay.

A very unusual memorial is the bridge built across a stream in Matterdale, Cumberland, in memory of Sir Cecil Spring Rice. He served as British Ambassador to the United States from 1914 to 1918 and helped greatly in bringing the countries closer together during those four fateful years.

In Holy Trinity Church, Stratford-on-Avon, there is an American window, paid for by contributions from American visitors, that depicts Amerigo Vespucci, Christopher Columbus, the landing of the Pilgrims, and William Penn.

The colonial clergyman, John Eliot, became known as the Apostle to the Indians because of his tremendous work among them, including the translating of the Bible and the Psalm Book into the Algonquin tongue. This was the first Bible printed in America. Eliot established communities of "praying Indians" who became invaluable allies to the colonists. Two-and-a-half centuries after his death in 1690, descendants of Eliot presented a six-light window to the Church of St. John the Baptist in Widford, Ware, Hertfordshire. In this small flint and stone church, Eliot had been baptized on August 5, 1604.

Sir Edwin Sandys, who died in 1629, was treasurer of the Virginia Company and drew up its constitution, which was used as a model by later colonies. Among other provisions, it stated that the people should be governed and taxed by their own consent, and should have an assembly modelled on the British House of Commons. Sir Edwin was buried in a Norman church in the village of Northbourne, just a mile from the city of Deal, on the Channel coast. In this squat little church, which looks something like a fortress, there is a large, ornate tomb to Sir Edwin and his wife. Beside the tomb, a table was erected by Americans in 1957, the 350th anniversary of the founding of Virginia. There is also a church memorial to Sandys in Scrooby, Nottinghamshire.

John Cabot, the Italian navigator who is credited with the discovery of the North American mainland, moved to London about 1484, after considerable experience at sea. He was encouraged by Henry VII to search for the Northwest Passage to the Orient. Cabot sailed from Bristol in 1497 and sighted the American coast at what is thought to be Cape Breton Island. He sailed again in 1498 and is thought to have reached Greenland and Baffin Island. England later based her claims to territory in North America on Cabot's discoveries. There is a fresco in the House of Commons showing Henry VII presenting John Cabot with a charter "to sail and explore westwards."

Vice-Admiral George Wilson Preedy successfully laid the first Atlantic cable, uniting Europe and America, when he was captain of the *Agamemnon.* Cooperating with an American frigate, the *Agamemnon* laid 335 miles of telegraph cable in 1857, but it soon broke. The following year the cable was successfully laid from Queenstown to Newfoundland, again with the cooperation of an American frigate. In the same church in East Budleigh, Devon, where Sir Walter Raleigh and his family worshipped, there is a memorial to Admiral Preedy.

Several other places in London, though strictly commercial, have close American ties. One is the firm of Davison, Newman and Company, at 52-58 Weston Street. They are the tea merchants whose tea was dumped into Boston Harbor on December 16, 1773. Through the years, the firm has cleverly turned this liability into an asset, by giving the brand name of "Boston Harbour Tea" to one of its finest blends and establishing a healthy market for its products along the east coast of America. In their headquarters there is a reproduction of one of the ill-fated ships.

The birthplace of the Liberty Bell should be a "must" for every American visitor to London. Now located at 34 Whitechapel Road in East London, this famous foundry was started in 1570 when Robert Mot began making bells. Through the years, several other foundries were bought up and incorporated, including the Gloucester Foundry, which was started in 1270. The Liberty Bell was cast at Whitechapel in 1752, was broken soon after it was hung, and was then recast in facsimile by Pass and Stow of Philadelphia. It was rung at the first public reading of the Declaration of Independence on July 8, 1776, and because of that eventful tolling, the bell was not recast when it finally cracked, while tolling the death of Chief Justice Marshall in 1835. Bellcasting is a highly specialized art that is practiced in only a few countries. In this foundry, one can see bells in all stages of production. The Whitechapel Foundry also cast Big Ben, the famous bell of Westminster.

Mme. Tussaud's famous waxworks, on Marlyebone Road, has dozens of figures and scenes relating to America's history, as well as portraying its heroes, innovators, and entertainers in all fields. Here you will find most of the presidents, as well as such illustrious characters as Lindbergh, Robert Frost, Dempsey, Valentino, Barnum, Drake, Franklin, Garbo, Goldwater, Shirley Temple, Gene Tunney, and dozens of others.

For more than three hundred years, the ties between Britain and America have been strengthened by intermarriage. Pocahontas, a genuine American, was the first to inaugurate this practice and it has been followed ever since. Undoubtedly the most famous Anglo-American marriage was that of Wallis Warfield Simpson and King Edward VIII, who gave up his throne in order "to marry the woman I love." The next most famous was that of Jennie Jerome and Lord Randolph Churchill, whose son Winston became Prime Minister during the fateful years after World War II. Another American beauty, Nancy Langhorne, married Waldorf Astor and became the first woman to take a seat as a member of Parliament. Such marriages played a definite role in the history of Great Britain, but there were many others, less famous but well worth noting.

The famous writer, Robert Louis Stevenson, born in Edinburgh, married an American woman when he was thirty years old. He met her in 1875 in the Fontainebleu district of France, where many artists then lived. Fanny Van de Grift Osbourne was then estranged from her husband and was trying to support herself as an artist. She was several years older than Stevenson, but he fell deeply in love with her. When she returned to the United States he followed her, despite his family's disapproval. Stevenson married Mrs. Osbourne in 1880, and in 1883 became reconciled with his family and he and his wife returned to Scotland. It is interesting to note that his first popular success as a writer of fiction came two years after his marriage to the American divorcee. The book which brought him fame, *Treasure Island,* was originally written for the amusement of his stepson, Lloyd Osbourne.

Another famous British writer, Rudyard Kipling, took an American bride, Caroline Balestier, and lived in Vermont for a number of years. For reasons of health, he and his wife spent the winters in South Africa for a number of years, where he became a friend of Theodore Roosevelt.

Other well known British writers, including Hilaire Belloc and H.G. Wells, had American wives. The famous British novelist George Eliot (Mary Ann Evans) married a New York banker, John Walter Cross, in 1880. In more recent years, the well known short story writer, Roald Dahl, married the famous American actress, Patricia Neal.

Averill Harriman, well known as an American financier and later as Ambassador to Soviet Russia and then to England, married Mrs. Pamela Churchill, the first wife of Randolph Churchill, who was Winston's only son.

The British nobility, no less than the writing profession, has often been attracted by the charms (and bank account?) of American women. The first wife of Lord Curzon, for example, was a daughter of Levi Leiter of Washington, D.C. The 11th Duke of Argyll, who died in 1973, had an American mother and went to school at Milton, Massachusetts before he entered Oxford. His fourth wife, Mrs. Mathilda Coster Mortimer, was an American. The Duke's daughter by his first wife became the wife of Norman Mailer, the American writer.

During the war years and immediately after, Anglo-American marriages were very common but they seldom made the headlines as did those mentioned above.

20

St. Paul's Cathedral and the American Memorial Chapel

For thirteen and a half centuries, a cathedral dedicated to the honor of St. Paul has stood upon the summit of Ludgate Hill in London. Sir Christopher Wren's great Renaissance church which rises majestically over the city is the fifth to bear the name of London's patron saint.

The story of St. Paul's begins in 604, when Mellitus was consecrated as Bishop of the East Saxons by St. Augustine of Canterbury. His cathedral, probably a wooden structure, was founded by Ethelbert, King of Kent, who endowed it with an estate in Essex which is still held by St. Paul's. This first cathedral was destroyed by fire, but was rebuilt in stone in 675-685 by Bishop Erkenwald. Throughout the Middle Ages, pilgrims came here to worship at the shrine of the saintly Bishop Erkenwald. This church was destroyed by the Vikings in the ninth century and rebuilt in 962.

In 1087, the stone church was burned down, but rebuilding was begun almost at once, with the support of William Rufus, son of William the Conqueror. Maurice, formerly chancellor to William the Conqueror, was now Bishop of London and he urged that a cathedral on a far vaster scale than anything previously done in London should be built. This cathedral, familiarly known as "Old St. Paul's," was the fourth church to be erected on the site. Built in the round-arched, Norman style, it stood within spacious precincts enclosed by walls with six gates, the principal one being on Ludgate Hill. Work on the choir was delayed by a fire in 1136 and it was not in use until 1148, when the remains of St. Erkenwald were taken to a new shrine behind the altar. The upper stages of the nave and the west end were completed by the end of the 12th century. This cathedral was finished and dedicated in 1240.

With a length of 596 feet, Old St. Paul's was the largest church in England. Only two churches in Europe surpassed it in size: the cathedrals in Seville and Milan. The spire, 489 feet high and the loftiest that had ever been built, was completed in 1315. In 1447 it was struck by lightning and not repaired until 1462. Surrounding the Norman cathedral itself were the bishop's palace, the deanery, and the homes of the residential canons. In 1335, a chapter house was built against the south side of the cathedral by William of Ramsey, one of the foremost architects of the day. Remains of the chapter house may still be seen in the gardens on the south side of the nave.

The most famous part of the precincts in the Middle Ages was Paul's Cross, an open-air pulpit which was the scene of many fiery sermons, especially during the Reformation. To the east lay the Cathedral School, which was refounded in 1512 by Dean Colet. This school, now well known as St. Paul's School, was transferred to Hammersmith in 1884.

The 14th century brought some splendid changes to the interior of the cathedral. The floors were paved with marble and the relics of St. Erkenwald, which were thought to work miracles, were laid in a more magnificent shrine adorned with gold.

During the early 15th century, St. Paul's was the

St. Paul's Cathedral, London.

setting for many trials for heresy and witchcraft. Those who were found guilty were taken from the Cathedral to nearby Smithfield to die by burning at the stake.

At the beginning of the 16th century, a state occasion of great magnificence was the marriage of Arthur, Prince of Wales, to Princess Catharine of Aragon. Within six months the ill-fated Catharine was a widow and seven years later she was quietly married at Greenwich to her brother-in-law, Henry VIII. Henry himself frequently attended services at Old St. Paul's on state occasions, as did Cardinal Wolsey, who was almost as resplendent a figure as the King himself.

During the Reformation instigated by Henry VIII, the churches were despoiled of their wealth and treasures and the services reduced to stark simplicity. St. Paul's was deprived not only of its wealth and treasures but much of its revenue as well. This lack of money was an important factor in the cathedral's later structural decay. Although some of the old ritual and glory were restored during the brief reign of Mary I, it was all suppressed when Elizabeth I ascended the throne. The Latin services were discontinued and the images which had been restored by Mary were quietly removed at night.

The new Protestant dean, Alexander Nowell, often preached before Elizabeth I. During the course of his sermon on Ash Wednesday, 1565, he attacked the use of images but was interrupted by the autocratic voice of his sovereign. "To your text, Mr. Dean, we have heard enough," called out Her Majesty.

After the Reformation, houses and shops were erected right up to the very walls of the Cathedral. The old practice of using the long nave, known as "Paul's Walk," as a passage-way and of conducting business there, grew to outrageous proportions. Services were held in the choir against the babble and chatter of tradespeople selling their wares and the noise of horses being led through the building. Despite protests, this practice continued until the end of the Norman cathedral and was even revived

148

St. Paul's at night.

for a time in 1724.

Shortly after Elizabeth I became queen, the spire of Old St. Paul's was struck by lightning on June 4, 1561, caught fire, and burned down to the roof which was badly damaged before the fire was put out. Repairs were begun at once and a temporary roof of boards and lead was put on. Three years later, Bishop Grindal re-roofed the transepts at his own expense, but no attempt was made to rebuild the spire.

Although a great service of thanksgiving was held on November 27, 1588, to celebrate England's victory over the Spanish Armada, the fire of 1561 and the poor roofing and hence inadequate protection against the weather all contributed to the deterioration of Old St. Paul's. Nothing was done, however, until 1628, when William Laud became bishop and Inigo Jones was appointed as King's Surveyor.

Jones immediately demolished the houses and shops that had been built up against the cathedral and made many changes in the church to improve its durability and its beauty. This work went on from 1634 until 1643, when the Civil War put a stop to building. The ravages of this war completed the deterioration which had begun with the fire of 1561. By the time Charles II was restored to the throne in 1660, Old St. Paul's was in the final stages of decay and deterioration. In the Great Fire of London in 1666, Old St. Paul's was completely destroyed.

It had been hoped that the Cathedral would escape the fire, and merchants had stored their goods in the churchyard and the crypt. But the raging flames leaped across from the burning buildings near by and set fire to the scaffolding around the tower of St. Paul's. Soon the entire building was ablaze and nothing remained unharmed but part of the walls and columns.

At first it was thought that the ruins could be restored, and the west end of the Cathedral was patched up for services in 1667, but when a column collapsed, it was obvious that a complete rebuilding would be necessary.

On July 2, 1668, Dean Sancroft wrote to the famous architect, Christopher Wren, asking him to prepare a design for submission to the King. In the next seven years, Wren submitted three designs. The third plan, which was finally accepted, was based on the Latin cross plan, calling for a nave much longer than the choir, with a domed crossing between nave and choir. There were to be shallow transepts and a western portico. This design was accepted by the King and the royal warrant was

149

issued in April, 1675, authorizing the design. It specifically allowed for "variations rather ornamental than essential," a provision that satisfied the commissioners.

When the site was cleared and the measurements taken, Wren asked a workman to bring him a stone so that he could mark the center of the new cathedral. The man brought a portion of a gravestone that was inscribed with the word *Resurgam* —"I shall rise again." Wren was so impressed that he had this word engraved on the exterior of the new cathedral, and it may be seen beneath the carved representation of a phoenix rising from the flames, in the pediment above the great south door.

The foundation stone was laid on June 21, 1675, but progress was slow. The choir was open for service in 1697, but members of the House of Commons were so dissatisfied with Wren's progress that they proposed that half his salary be withheld until the cathedral was completed. It was not until 1711, after personally petitioning Queen Anne, that Wren received the full amount due him.

By 1698 the main part of the cathedral was completed, and the last stone at the apex of the lantern above the cupola was placed in position by Sir Christopher Wren's son in 1708. It was now forty-two years since the Great Fire, but Wren had the satisfaction of seeing his masterpiece completed during his lifetime. He made frequent visits to the great cathedral and after one such visit on a cold day in February, 1723, he died quietly in his chair in his home at Hampton Court, at the age of ninety-one. Sir Christopher Wren was buried in the crypt of St. Paul's.

Wren was a genius in choosing the able artists and craftsmen of his day, and it is inside the cathedral that their work can be best appreciated. During World War II, St. Paul's suffered two direct hits from high explosive bombs. One of these penetrated the choir roof and completely destroyed the High Altar and damaged the Victorian marble reredos. St. Paul's was also attacked by incendiary bombs, but the devoted band of fire-watchers extinguished them before they caused too much damage. Essential repairs were carried out after the bombing, but the postwar task of restoration was a tremendous one. The new High Altar, consecrated on May 7, 1958, is the British people's memorial to those of the Commonwealth who lost their lives in the war.

St. Paul's is more than a magnificent feat of architecture and the resting place of the great and famous. It is first and foremost a place where worship is offered to God every day, with all the richness of music and ceremonial that is possible. St. Paul's is, after all, London's cathedral.

Of greatest interest to American visitors, however, is the American Memorial Chapel in St. Paul's. The United States Army Air Force erected upon its airfields in Britain small memorial tablets to those who had given their lives in battle. In 1945, they asked the late Lord Trenchard if he could help them to find a site for a central memorial in London. He replied, "It is not for you but for us to erect that memorial." As president of the American and British-Commonwealth Association, Lord Trenchard urged that group to sponsor such a memorial. He and his associates decided that the most fitting memorial would be a chapel in one of Britain's great cathedrals. Dr. W.R. Matthews, Dean of St. Paul's, suggested that the memorial should be in St. Paul's Cathedral.

When told of the plan, General Eisenhower was deeply moved and offered to cooperate by providing a Roll of Honor with the names of those whose memory the chapel was intended to enshrine. With the full support of King George VI, a drive for funds was launched on November 15, 1945, by means of letters in the *Times* and *The Daily Telegraph.* These letters, which asked for money to provide, furnish, and endow the Chapel in St. Paul's, were widely copied by other newspapers throughout the country. There was an immediate response from all sections of the community, ranging from checks from wealthy corporations to pennies from children in an orphanage. With the cooperation of the movie industry, which presented a film on the subject and collected funds from movie-goers, a total of £57,616 was raised. It could be truly said that the Chapel was built with the pennies and sixpences provided by several million people of the United Kingdom.

The United States services provided a list of more than 28,000 Americans who would be memorialized in the great Cathedral where Nelson and the Duke of Wellington are buried. These names were all written by hand, with details of rank and service, on 473 pieces of vellum. In one of its opening pages, the Roll of Honor states that it contains "the names of those Americans serving with the Canadian, British, and United States

The American Memorial Chapel in St. Paul's.

Armed Forces who gave their lives while enroute to or while stationed in the United Kingdom. It also includes those members of units permanently based in the United Kingdom who made the supreme sacrifice between D-Day and VE-Day."

On July 4, 1951, at a memorable service in a packed Cathedral and in the presence of the Queen and the two Princesses (King George VI being unable to attend because of illness), General Eisenhower presented this Roll of Honor to the Dean of St. Paul's.

The extreme east end of the Cathedral had been chosen as the site for the Chapel. An entirely new High Altar of marble was erected, with a carved oak canopy upheld by twelve oak pillars and resting on white marble pedestals. Thus the lower part of the chapel is screened by the High Altar but the central window of the Chapel, which is the chief stained-glass window of the Cathedral, can be seen by worshippers entering through the main west door. The marble pedestal bearing the Roll of Honor backs upon the High Altar and stands under the shelter of the canopy. No finer site could have been found in all Britain.

After years of loving care and thought, the Chapel was finished and furnished with a beauty and splendor far greater than anticipated when it was first conceived. The Chapel was dedicated at a moving ceremony on November 26, 1958, with Queen Elizabeth II and other members of the Royal Family, as well as the then Vice-President, Richard M. Nixon, in attendance. The Bishop of

The American Memorial Chapel in St. Paul's.

London conducted the service, consecrating the Chapel altar and blessing its crucifix and candlesticks. The Queen herself unveiled the inscription below the Roll of Honor and trumpets sounded "Taps," followed, after a pause, by "Reveille." Throughout the service the American flag stood beside the High Altar of London's great Cathedral.

The Chapel may be entered through gates of wrought iron, painted in black and gold. The floor is of black and white Italian marble, in a design showing two five-pointed stars. Inlaid in the floor is the inscription: "To the American dead of the Second World War, from the people of Britain." The walls of the Chapel are lined with oak, up to the windows, and on either side of the chapel altar are six carved oak stalls. The Roll of Honor is contained in a case of glass and gold resting upon a marble pedestal which stands on the rear steps of

the High Altar of the Cathedral. The pedestal is inscribed in golden letters: "This Chapel commemorates the common sacrifices of the British and American peoples during the Second World War and especially those American service men whose names are recorded in its Roll of Honor. This tablet was unveiled by Her Majesty Queen Elizabeth II on 26 November, 1958, in the presence of Richard M. Nixon, the Vice-President of the United States of America."

The three windows of the Memorial Chapel, each twenty-two feet high, are designed to represent the service, sacrifice, and resurrection of the Christian soldier in terms of Biblical scenes from the life of Christ. Each window has an appropriate border consisting of the insignia of the states and territories of the United States and of the U.S. Army and Navy.

The altar rails are of the finest wrought iron, decorated in black and gold to match the gates. The altar cross and candlesticks are of silver heavily plated with gold. The cross stands four feet, two inches high and weighs 525 ounces. The candlesticks are two feet, three inches high and weigh 403 ounces each.

After the ceremony of dedication and while the congregation of three thousand sang the inspiring "Battle Hymn of the Republic," the procession returned from the Memorial Chapel to the body of the Cathedral for the address by the Dean. He spoke of "the new treasure in our historic building that, in a deeper sense, may remind many generations of the common effort and common sacrifices of the two great English-speaking peoples and fill them with the determination to keep that comradeship alive and vigorous." He prayed that this comradeship might go on and that peace and justice may be established not only for our two peoples but for all the nations of the earth.

Index